Provocations

Provocations

drew Plunkett

The work of david connor

LUND HUMPHRIES

First published in 2020 by Lund Humphries

Lund Humphries
Office 3, Book House
261A City Road
London EC1V 1JX
UK

www.lundhumphries.com

Provocations: The Work of David Connor
© Drew Plunklett and David Connor, 2020
All rights reserved

Drawings, unless otherwise indicated, © David Connor, 2020. All rights reserved

ISBN: 978-1-84822-351-6

A Cataloguing-in-Publication record for this book is available from the British Library

All rights reserved. No part of this publication may be reproduced, stored in a retrieval system or transmitted in any form or by any means, electrical, mechanical or otherwise, without first seeking the permission of the copyright owners and publishers. Every effort has been made to seek permission to reproduce the images in this book. Any omissions are entirely unintentional, and details should be addressed to the publishers.

Drew Plunkett has asserted his right under the Copyright, Designs and Patent Act, 1988, to be identified as the Author of this Work.

Printed in Slovenia

Cover: Vittoriale Project in Roppongi, Tokyo, restaurants and night club. David Connor (drawing) design with Julian Powell-Tuck, PTCO.
Cover design by David Connor

One – Beginnings 7

Two – The Middle 69

Three – Not The End 95

Four – Paean 146

Notes 148

Important teachers 150

Collaborators 150

Image credits 150

Index 151

David Connor at Burlington Lodge Studios, London, 1979.

beginnings

In the second half of the 1970s Britain was in crisis, destabilised by industrial disputes and economic recession and ready for change. Architecture and design were dealing with their own crisis. Ur-Modernism was running out of credibility. In 1977, Charles Jencks, in *The Language of Post-Modern Architecture*, produced a taxonomy of its dissenting strands and gave them respectability. Radical change was in the ether and it was neatly reflected in a volte-face in youth culture. Nihilistic punks of the 1970s were superseded by narcissistic New Romantics, the pioneers of the preening, prosperous and Postmodernist 1980s.

David Connor knew all about Postmodernism and, if he was just a little too old to engage sartorially with either punk or New Romanticism, he was in tune with the former's iconoclasm, the latter's subversive retrospection and the provocative self-expression of both. With two small interiors projects in 1981 and 1982, one broadly punk and one broadly New Romantic, he bewildered established interior design practitioners and energised their successors – those who were still students but would go on to transform the interiors of British high streets and the tastes of those who used them. In 1984, with the same recklessness he tackled his first major architectural project, for a grand country house in California. With no formal architectural training he brought very little philosophical baggage to that task and demonstrated how boisterous reinterpretation of precedents could produce something that was disconcertingly new.

His first published projects established him as a creative contrarian, congenitally disinclined to align with others or indeed to repeat himself. Unlike other leading figures he has not, over 40 years of practice, evolved a signature style. The constant in his creative processes is his readiness to understand each project's particularities and to find a bespoke solution for it. He immerses himself in the opportunity each project offers and looks for something particular to it. That implied objectivity may suggest something close to the dour old definition of design as a problem-solving exercise, and he does plan meticulously, but he builds on those bare bones, to overlay prosaic efficiency with evocative flourishes that provoke the imagination and emotions.

He has stirred the imaginations and ambitions of young designers perhaps as much with his drawings as with his projects. He has demonstrated, if not an entirely new way of finding and evolving ideas, a new way of visualising them that has led him, and his acolytes, far beyond conventional solutions. He pays lip service to the laws of perspective but concentrates on explaining the experience of being in the space he is proposing.

The published drawings that helped make his reputation look like sketches made at an advanced point in the creative process; but they are more retrospective than that, made for presentations to clients to explain the experience he was offering and, given the backgrounds and predilections of his earliest clients, they struck the right note. When commissioning Connor one was not looking for a conventional professional service.

Putting it on paper

Projects begin with drawings and drawing is a good place to start if one is to understand the nature of Connor's creativity. His drawings come from his art college training, where the subjective and therefore self-indulgent gesture is valued over the objective, rather than from an architectural training where rational analysis and dogma set the agenda. The drawings he made early to pin down first thoughts were, apart from their uninhibited content, little different from those of other designers.

It was those made later in the process, and particularly for clients, that reflected his particular way of seeing and presenting his particular visions. At the beginning of the 1980s his monochromatic skewed perspectives were the antithesis of prevailing practice. They had decidedly more in common with the images of 1920s German Expressionist cinema. His drawings, and particularly the figures who inhabit them, look undisputedly decadent. Men in evening dress with monocles have the faces of German Expressionist vampires; women wear the black gowns and plunging necklines of John Singer Sargent's *Madame X* and offer glimpses of their square nipples. They were, like him, punks with New Romantic sensibilities.

However uninhibited the drawings may be they were, and remain, reference points throughout the process of translating vision into reality, ensuring that conceptual ambition is not diluted. They were first published and exhibited at the onset of the 1980s and gave hope and confidence to the young designers whose worth and future were being questioned by proselytisers for the computer who suggested that it would replace the human for strategic and tactical creative thinking. His drawings

Villa Zapu 1984, Napa, California: an early sketch setting out the location of elements on site.

confirmed what creative spirits suspected; that originality relied on the possibilities thrown up by and spotted by wayward human imaginations in the process of making thoughts tangible.

Before Connor, the conventions for visual representation were formulaic but the formula worked and was taught as an essential professional skill on Interior Design courses. Since most of these were located in art schools, the making of mechanically constructed three-dimensional drawings seemed a tedious process and tended to alienate those students with freer spirits, those most likely to be innovative. Connor did not quarrel with the conventions of two-dimensional drawings, recognising that there is no better way to examine and communicate the hard facts from which a project will be constructed. It was his three-dimensional drawings that upset matters.

The perspective view was the established method of seducing a client. Conventional practice required its setting up by mechanical means and that it should be coloured by watercolour, gouache or felt-tip pen. Graphic facility was confused with creativity. The skills needed to make such images were hard to master and required continuous practice. To ensure standards were upheld, commercial practices bought in the expertise of professional perspective artists, or 'visualisers', whose work had the benefit of well-rehearsed

Adam Ant's country house: two drawings made for the client that show the expressionistic disregard for formal perspective and the 'Nosferatu' figures that characterise Connor's drawing.

expertise but carried the mark of the visualiser rather than the designer.

Constructed perspective gave equal weight to all elements within an interior and ignored the reality – that one's eye flitted around the space and alighted on the things that caught one's attention. Connor demonstrated how one could emphasise what was important and that explaining a proposal was about much more than technique or medium or literal representation. Students, about to become fledgling professionals, rushed to emulate him. They wanted to draw what they thought rather than what the users of their interiors might be presumed to see. They were in art schools and wanted to be seen as artistic rather than dully professional. Forty years on, when computer software offers the ability to draw and render with photographic realism, the more ambitious continue to prioritise depiction of atmosphere.

Connor's drawings were blatantly personal. They had the vigour of spontaneity and seemed to embody creative energy. He seldom used colour and when he did it was rarely more than a line or an isolated patch and it was never bright. Once at a lecture when asked why his drawings had no colour he gave the unnecessarily cryptic answer that he considered them to be 'full of colour'. It was hardly a satisfactory answer in the circumstances and perhaps with more time to reflect he would have elaborated and explained that, for him, the missing colours were there – in his mind's eye. It could also be said that, when he made the comment, his projects tended to be monochromatic.

Whatever questions might be asked about monochrome drawings, there is no doubt that his drawings excited clients, perhaps because they smacked not of the mechanised art of the professional visualiser but the anarchy of the artist. Connor was not adverse to this perception. At the beginning of the 1980s, when there was suddenly a popular enthusiasm for interior design, a popularity for which his work more than that of any others was responsible, his drawings were exhibited with the pomp and circumstance conventionally associated with fine art. He enjoyed the kudos and his extraordinary, and bizarre, images were validated by the projects they set in motion. They affirmed the importance of the aberrant human imagination and suggested that design, whether of interiors or exteriors, could, and probably should, be a medium for self-expression, that the more personal the vision the greater its impact would be. It was a message that students were delighted to hear and they learnt that an interior relied for its impact, not on its adherence to the rules of perspective construction, but on its atmosphere, its mood. The spontaneity of his drawings – and their personality – can suggest frivolity but as he draws his way further into a project he becomes increasingly and seriously absorbed in its particularities and the possibilities inherent in them.

His sketches examine both conceptual strategies and detailing tactics. Nick Coombe, immediately after graduating from the RCA and before setting up his own practice, worked with Connor in the early 1980s and remembers how he would pin quintessential sketches, usually less developed than those he chose to publish, around the workspace as a reminder to his team, and himself, of the priorities that were to be adhered to. Coombe remembers him saying, 'We too are artists. Through our work we are also reflecting on the human condition.'[1] Coombe also remembers him as a 'good planner'[2] who would work to organise the layout of rooms, to ensure an efficient deployment of furniture, which in its turn could determine how he located less functional elements. Given that his rooms were performances in their own right it is clear that this creation of interaction between elements was crucial. One could speculate that his early experience working with the high society decorator John Stefanidis would have taught him the importance of precision. Society clients expect their decorators not only to buy artefacts on their behalf but to mark their very precise location: maids need to know exactly where to replace them after dusting. Connor did not have that kind of client but he understood the importance of precisely maximising impact.

Drawing has obviously been more to him than a means to explore and communicate ideas. He necessarily made the exploratory drawings that every designer must and which end in waste bins. The highly wrought and comprehensively, if idiosyncratically, completed drawings he made beyond that point were nominally for presentation to clients but their number and the intensity suggest that they went beyond necessity. They were opportunities to relish his ideas. He could have made conventional perspective views and coloured them neatly and conscientiously and clients would have accepted them as the inevitable norm. It takes the courage of obsession to subvert the normal way of doing things but he had clients who were themselves re-writing conventional practices. He was lucky to fall in with them.

The drawings were the clearest expressions of his obsessions. He did them because, no matter how faithfully his instructions were followed, the finished buildings and interiors could never match the wildly contorted, mildly perverted, worlds he was dreaming up. The drawings allowed him to take his ideas into spaces bigger than any he was asked to conceive, spaces that were unfettered by the limitations of building materials or techniques and that were inhabited by the strange and exotically sinister creatures he drew. They allowed him to inhabit his visions by proxy.

Hull City of Culture 2017: speculative drawings for an installation at Hull Minster.

Hull City of Culture, 2017: an interior for the temporary housing, complete with expressionistic perspective and vampiric presence.

When he made them he was in the throes of his obsessions. His professional partner, Julian Powell-Tuck, remembers that he would often begin the drawing with one of these figures in the foreground, his alter ego staring at him as he drew. The creatures did not represent the client but they were the people he thought his clients ought to become when they inhabited the homes he made for them.

There are designers whose work is instantly recognisable, individuals who are in thrall to an idea, a material or a construction technique. The best of them refine their basics and leave their imitators far behind. Then there are others, ultimately more interesting, who have no obvious stylistic tics; those whose work proclaims quality but not its author. Good designers do not repeat themselves; they find something unique in the briefs they are given. Those who chose to repeat their tricks become caricatures of themselves. Connor appears to be genetically predisposed not to repeat himself. It is possible to see similarities between elements in several projects but these occur most obviously in early sketches when interests, and sometimes obsessions, that lurk at the back of his imagination pop up when he moves to a new project and, as he digs his way more deeply below the surface of existing site and brief, he finds something appropriately particular to it.

The way he makes drawings remains constant and while they remain constantly and instantly recognisable, the buildings that have resulted from them have defied attribution. His graphic consistency perhaps represents the uninhibited thinking process that always finds something uniquely particular for each brief. His projects display no visual tics.

Early days

Connor was born in 1950, in Birmingham, the second eldest of four children. During the Second World War his father enlisted as a soldier and, 'because he was bright', was posted to Washington, D.C., to work on the Lend-Lease scheme, the shipping of supplies and arms from the United States to Britain and Russia in discreet support of their fight against Germany.[3] His mother was Swiss, born into a family of cheesemakers that moved first to France and then to England, where they set up a factory in Wiltshire. She took out British citizenship and, during the Second World War, worked in aircraft factories and as a land girl.

Once demobbed, his father won a scholarship to Oxford. When he graduated, still enamoured of academic life, he found a job at Birmingham University setting up, and running for the rest of his working life, the Extra Mural Department, to encourage and support academic ambition and achievement beyond secondary school level for those too old to have taken advantage of post-war educational reforms. Connor describes him as 'an atheist, socialist, republican'[4] and suggests that his own attitudes are still influenced by those principles, which might be lumped together as 'iconoclastic' – which is perhaps the word that best describes his processes and his projects. His mother worked as a teacher before succumbing to the responsibilities of raising four children.

In 1953 the family moved to Bourneville, the model village originally built by the philanthropic Cadbury family to house the workers in their chocolate factory. One might argue convincingly that the village's lavishly landscaped grounds and picturesque Arts and Crafts architecture had a discernable influence on Connor, and certainly the quality and visual richness of his environment could only have tuned his eye to high standards and encouraged his instinct to shirk compromise. If the Cadburys, who belonged to the benign Quaker sect, were keen to foster the spiritual well-being of their workers, they also promoted health and fitness. Bourneville had, within its 120 acres, generous parks and sports provision, which may have encouraged the Connor parents to move there. Both were sporting. His mother played tennis and his father cricket, both at county level. Connor denies having sporting prowess but even latent sporting genes can encourage competitive instincts and the courage to take risks, which are assets when one is proposing and realising radical ideas.

In the 1950s, as Connor was growing up, Britain was only beginning to emerge from the period of rationing and austerity that had followed the war. Birmingham had been the second-most-bombed city after London, and its centre was still dotted with bomb sites and the ruins of houses and factories. Bourneville was a retreat. The Connors lived in a large semi-detached house, built in the best Bournevillian Arts and Crafts manner. Connor walked along tree-lined streets to his primary school, another Arts and Crafts building. His classroom was in the bell tower, which shook as the bells rang out every hour. It was an environment that could only stimulate the imagination.

Learning

Connor remembers a few childhood experiences that he believes have had some influence on his work. His father read to him from a book of Norse legends, which were illustrated by romantic black-and-white etchings. Each illustration was protected by tissue paper, which made the turning of a page a notable event. The images were 'full of action, sea monsters, Vikings and maidens in distress'.[5] He was equally excited by Birmingham Art Gallery's considerable collection of Pre-

Raphaelite paintings, attracted by their wealth of detail and exotic historicism – and by the fact that they each told a story.

When he was 16 he volunteered to change slides for a colleague of his father who was delivering weekly lectures for adults on the history of European art, from the Renaissance to the 20th century. Across that historic spectrum he was most impressed by the German Expressionists and the Italian Futurists, concluding that 'they were having the most fun', as they distorted perspective and splashed colours.[6]

Connor was dyslexic so, in 1969, found himself in the Birmingham School of Art rather than at university. It is acknowledged that dyslexics often have strong visual skills. The disproportionate percentage to be found in art schools suggests that to be true and the condition is considered to increase understanding of three-dimensional form. Under-performance in institutionalised examinations is a distinction shared by many innovators in creative fields who tend not to be the sort of swots who answer all the questions and consequently end up in architecture schools. Connor managed to achieve the lowest grade in his A level art examination. Fortunately in the 1960s and 1970s recruiters in art schools chose to be unimpressed by grades and liked to think they could spot quirky talents. His subsequent career might be seen as a memorial to the success of recruitment outside the box.

After a general first year course sampling a gamut of disciplines and some uncertainty about the specialism he should pursue he decided, after considering theatre set design, to join the Interior Design Department. Within art schools the subject was then not a glamorous choice. Few knew what it was about, or what it could be about, but, at the time he was making his decision Britain was 'swingin', shaped by a sudden national obsession with pop music and tawdry fashion. Design, in one form or another, was seen as the facilitator of chic and chic needed new environments.

The transition from post-war austerities to 1960s frivolities began in the 1950s, precipitated by 1951's Festival of Britain. In its wake brightly coloured plastics, splayed spindly legs on chairs and tables, and decorative borrowings from scientific diagrams characterised and popularised progressive British interior design. By the mid-1960s interior design was creeping into the kind of newspapers and magazines that an academic household, such as the Connors, would take. Fashion in interiors became volatile and the 1960s rushed to find an aesthetic that was clearly not of the 1950s: furniture became solid and well-rounded, white replaced bright. The Habitat furniture chain was offering the components for a progressive lifestyle that fused mild modernity and the artefacts of Mediterranean peasants. After music and fashion, interior design was the essential factor in a progressive lifestyle and it was encountered in fashionable cafes: Way In, with its globular plastic chairs opened on the top floor of Harrods and the Drugstore on the King's Road in Chelsea was characterised by huge semi-circular and quadrant curves cut into shiny aluminium cladding inside and out. King's Road was the most fashionable street in Chelsea and therefore the most fashionable street in London, which was, with the possible exception of Paris, the most fashionable city in the world. In design, and every other facet of life, change for change's sake was mandatory.

Finding his place

Art schools were seen as appropriate environments for youths inclined to be rebellious and 1968, the year before Connor began art school, had been a particularly fractious year. In Paris, French students initiated riots that came close to destroying the government. They made revolution chic as they dug up and hurled cobblestones at police and pasted up elegant black-and-white posters across the city. Their British counterparts could not resist following suit but, with more limited political nous, could only pick quarrels about the content of their curricula. In art schools established presumptions, deemed elitist, about aesthetics were called into question but the insurgents had little of coherence to offer in their place and they were not fighting the forces of reaction. Art schools were in thrall to Modernity, and the Bauhaus was held to be the epitome of progressive artistic thought and a model for any progressive art institution. Connor learnt about its leading lights, painters like Kandinsky and Klee, architects like Gropius and Mies van der Rohe. He was also introduced to Russian Constructivists like Malevich and Rodchenko. The last two were particularly admired amongst revolting students for their socialist credentials, which chimed well with the smattering of leftist aspirations borrowed from the more sophisticated French. Connor recognised the importance of the Bauhaus and its leading lights in the invention of the modern world but, to his credit, considered them to have become the prevailing orthodoxy and that it was the job of his generation to 'move the conversation on'.[7]

Rather than browse library volumes devoted to Le Corbusier and Mies van der Rohe he bought books on, amongst other esoteric topics, medieval castles, tree houses and concrete wartime bunkers. He was 'trying to find an existing architecture that might lead to something new'.[8] His favourite house was Adalberto Libera's Villa Malaparte, the strange step-roofed dwelling that seems to emerge organically from a cliff top on the isle of Capri. His second favourite was Eileen Gray's E-1027, built on another rocky Mediterranean coast and considered to be a better realisation of Le Corbusier's principles than anything Corbusier himself achieved. Gray had disagreed with Corbusier's dictum that a house should be a 'machine for living in' and counter-declared that it should be a 'living organism', a reflection of the evolving lives of those who lived in it.[9] It is significant that Connor was drawn to her project. In his best work, which is primarily residential, there is a quality that recognises the particularity of his clients' personae and nudges them towards pursuing it further.

As he settled into his interior design course Connor was impressed by the work of Max Clendinning, then the leading progressive British interior designer who had throughout the 1960s specialised in white rooms, curving corners and melding the planes of walls and ceilings. He remembers being excited by the internal landscape of Ronnie Scott's jazz club, an amphitheatre of stacked serpentine steps, high enough to act as seating for the audience. He was learning from film set design and in particular the cool grey interiors of *2001: A Space Odyssey*. He liked them because 'they wrapped around you, every surface was designed'.[10] He was thinking of the circular rooms which, in zero gravity, allowed the astronauts to stroll effortlessly up walls and along ceilings. It was an aesthetic far away from the lumpy Brutalist concrete that characterised the architecture that was appearing around him in the rebuilding of Birmingham's city centre. The comic book imagery of a metallic future may have inspired the new student but when he came to practice ten years later he had lost interest in the weightlessness of space and preferred the weightlessness of allusion.

While now conceding that 'Bourneville was nice to grow up in'[11] he was keen to leave Birmingham, which never managed to match the fashionable reputations of other provincial cities like Liverpool and Manchester. It may have been too much of the Midlands, perceived to be lacking fashionable northern grit. He wanted to get to 'strange and exotic' London, the epicentre of global youth culture.[12] He was accepted for the Masters course in Interior Design at the Royal College of Art, which was then a unique institution, the only exclusively postgraduate art school in Britain. It recruited few students and offered kudos, by association, to its alumni, which eased their way to professional success. The College, as it was referred to by its blasé graduates, had a reputation for glamour that bolstered alumni's confidence. They were not expected, nor did they expect, to be journeymen or journeywomen.

The course was headed by Sir Hugh Casson who as architectural director of the Festival of Britain had led the crusade to whet the British public's appetite for modernity. The College had been keen to set up an architectural course but was thwarted by the Royal Institute of British Architects' judgment that the resources of a small specialist department within a multi-disciplinary institution would be unable to support a viable curriculum. At 41 years old, Sir Hugh was already becoming an architectural grandee but perhaps his credentials for establishing a serious new school of architecture were undermined by the enormous popularity of the Festival and its association with an easy-going version of Modernism that palpably lacked the gravitas that architects expected of their pedagogy.

Sir Hugh's wife, Lady Margaret, was head tutor and the three year long course was conducted with elegant informality. (When the RCA bursar complained about a jazz band rehearsing in the interior design studio, Sir Hugh explained that 'designers could not possibly work without jazz'.)[13] To be taught by such personages could not fail to have an effect on a Brummie. Connor remembers being taken to lunch in the senior common room by Sir Hugh and remembers being impressed by ice-cooled butter dishes, three RCA branded wines and the copies of David Hockney's self-generated degree certificate that decorated the walls.

(Hockney had not bothered to go through the examination processes but the College was keen to recognise its celebrated alumnus. Connor was reassured that wayward talent was applauded.)

At a time when no one was quite sure what interior design should be, Sir Hugh, who had unexpectedly found himself a cheerleader for the discipline, wrote in 1966 a definitive essay of the subject. It was called 'Inscape' and in it he argued that the clue to understanding interior design was contained in the decadent fin-de-siècle aesthete Robert de Montesquiou's pronouncement that 'an apartment is a mood'.[14] Perhaps Casson spotted a decadence in Connor or perhaps a tendency to think about interiors in a Montesquiou-esque way and thought a conversation over lunch would be useful. Connor only remembers his struggle with the cutlery.

When the Cassons moved on in 1974, in Connor's second year, the course leadership passed to a commoner, but one who was a distinguished architect for all that. John Millar was encouraged to provide the academic evidence that would persuade the Royal Institute of British Architects (RIBA) to allow the institution to award postgraduate architectural degrees. The course changed its name to Environmental Design and took on a distinctly architectural character. There was growing awareness of 'environmental' concerns (the

Ecologist magazine had been founded in 1970) but the word had no particular ecological connotations. For the RCA it was a way to circumvent the legal restriction on the use of the word architecture while allowing the course to spread its pedagogic wings. There was an increased bias towards large-scale architectural projects and head tutor Ed Jones described it as an 'architecture course manqué'.[15] It refrained from burdening its small coterie of students who were often from the diverse, un-architectural backgrounds of interior and furniture design with comprehensive lectures on building construction. It was presumed that a strategic overview of constructional theory would prepare them to learn necessary practical skills in practice. Unburdened by concerns about passing technical examinations the students became adept at winning competitions against established and well-regarded schools of architecture and the course quickly became recognised as providing a strong grounding in conceptual and strategic thinking. The practical deficiency was partly the result of limited staffing resources, as the RIBA had predicted, and partly because the majority of students, like Connor, lacked an appropriate undergraduate grounding in building construction. Julian Powell-Tuck who became Connor's business partner, gave the department's standard line of defence in an interview for the *RIBA Journal* explaining that

'There's a lot you learn as you go along . . . what really matters is learning to design.'[16] Which is largely true; the niceties of building construction are not learnt in lecture theatres but when fledgling architects find themselves obliged to deal with unpleasantries on site. And of course graduates left the RCA with carapaces of self-confidence.

Connor remains unaccountably proud of having been voted Miss RCA in the 1973 drag contest and, in that guise, gracing the cover of the college's magazine.

Practising

When he graduated, and after a number of short-term contracts, Connor found his first steady job with John Stefanidis. There he became acclimatised to the idea of working on projects with extravagant budgets, using esoteric materials and arcane techniques. Had he stayed he might have evolved into a conventional, if racy, decorator. But it is doubtful.

RCA graduates tended to be a tight-knit community. Ben Kelly, who had graduated the year before Connor, was aware of his work and perhaps more importantly his approach to design. Kelly designed a rehearsal room for the Sex Pistols punk band and a 'shag pad' for its guitarist Steve Jones.[17] The Pistols' *éminence*

'Seditionaries Redux', from the exhibition *Punk: Chaos to Culture*, 2013, Metropolitan Museum of Art, New York. The museum reconstruction, viewed from beyond the fourth wall, does not quite convey the sinister ad hoc charm of the original small shop.

'Seditionaries Redux', from the exhibition *Punk: Chaos to Culture*, 2013, Metropolitan Museum of Art, New York. Facsimiles of the collaged images of bombed-out Dresden that decorated the walls of the original shop.

grise, Malcolm McLaren then asked Kelly to remodel the front of the shop at 430 King's Road where he and his partner Vivienne Westwood sold clothes to the youth cult of the moment. McLaren and Westwood were relentlessly entrepreneurial and transformed the shop at regular intervals. In 1976 they wanted to change the name from SEX to Seditionaries, for the punk market they were nurturing. Kelly gave them milky glass windows, metal grilles and a flickering fluorescent tube. It could have been the frontage of a failing plumbers merchant. It was and was meant to be intimidating. Robert Elms, in his sartorial autobiography *The Way We Wore: A Life in Threads*, writes of the moments of anxiety he experienced as an aspirant punk before steeling himself to enter.

McLaren and Westwood wanted the interior to be decorated with images of bomb-damaged Dresden and asked Kelly to make some sketches. Kelly did not like working to order and suggested that they employ Connor, whose drawing style was better suited to the task. Kelly and Connor met in a cafe to discuss the project and Kelly left on a planned trip to New York. McLaren was putting most of his energy into promoting the Sex Pistols and Connor worked primarily with Westwood but found McLaren's modus operandi inspirational and liberating.

After society decorating, Connor welcomed the opportunity to work directly with an anarchic, if opinionated, client and was given an insight into a territory in which an interior designer might operate that was at the opposite pole from that of Stefanidis. He has described McLaren as a 'genius'[18] and was happy to implement, and contribute to, his ideas. It was hands-on work and he found himself surrounded by exponents of the startlingly new punk clothes, who worked in or lounged around the shop. His primary task was to make a collage of black-and-white photographs of the bombed ruins of Dresden and he added his own inverted image of Piccadilly Circus. He was impressed when McLaren punched a hole in the suspended ceiling, to suggest bomb damage, and then suspended a naked light bulb through it. (It has since been suggested that the cancer that killed McLaren 30 years later was caused by the asbestos he was exposed to during that 'refurbishment'.) Connor became mildly obsessed with punk and was happy to supplement his £30 fee with a selection of Westwood garments, including a shirt with a discreet swastika motif that he carelessly wore on a visit to Berlin. It was not such a bad deal. Westwood's punk garments did not come cheap and he now regrets that when he later stored the collection at his parents' house, his mother failed to recognise their net worth and put them in the bin.

Seditionaries was catering for a niche market and, apart from its punk customers, went unseen and unappreciated. It did receive

Seditionaries, King's Road, London: a surviving photograph of the original shop showing the inverted image of Piccadilly Circus.

Worlds End, London: an early Connor proposal for reworking the facade of Seditionaries.

Worlds End, London: Connor's final proposal that suggested the tile hanging, the blue window and, most significantly, the huge clock with its backward-racing hands that were the essence of the expurgated built version.

a considerable 'posthumous' accolade in 2013 when the Metropolitan Museum of Art in New York recreated the interior for its exhibition *Punk: Chaos to Culture*. Connor provided information and advice on the replication.

His contribution to Seditionaries was enough to convince both McLaren and Westwood that he was equipped to change the facade when they later decided to revamp and rename the shop. It became World's End, which was also the name of the unsalubrious section of the King's Road on which it stood; but the name suited the fey fatalistic New Romantics and the restyled premises were to cater for them, the next targets for McLaren's entrepreneurial attentions. Unlike punks, who were a McLaren creation, New Romantics had evolved independently as a camp fashion cult for those desperate to move on from punk's tattiness. If punks wore rags and 'pogoed' on the spot with flailing arms, New Romantics dressed up with parodic glamour and danced languidly and offered a new and more productive territory for Westwood, who had made her initial mark with torn T-shirts and bondage trousers for punks, to work in and move towards the more rarefied uplands of couture.

Connor produced three proposals for the facade. The drawings were characteristic expressionistic impressions, but each included a clock, about 2 m in diameter, the hands of which would sweep backwards at a brisk pace. It alluded to *Alice's Adventures in Wonderland*. None of the proposals were built. It may have been that McLaren suspected they might be too expensive or he may have already turned his attention to cooking up a new youth cult to which he could sell Westwood's clothes, and was undecided about exactly what that might look like. Perhaps he had his own ideas at the back of his mind and Connor's were wide of that mark. Whatever the reason, Connor was surprised some time later when passing the shop to see what looked like a multi-paned, 18th century bow-fronted shop window, crowned by a panel of vertically hung slates with, at their centre, a very large clock, the hands of which raced backwards; a hybrid of *Old Curiosity Shop* and *Alice*. Inside, the floor sloped, as Connor had proposed. In later publications the design has been attributed to McLaren, Westwood and a few assistants but conceptually it was Connor's. The clock remained true to his intention and had he been involved in the project's completion the slates and the shop window would have been delivered with far greater aplomb.

He had other significant connections with both punk and New Romanticism. When the creators of the Roxy, an important punk venue, moved on to New Romanticism with the Fridge in Brixton he provided them with concept drawings.

Footholds

Connor was establishing himself outside the well-mannered world of Stefanidis and his professional circumstances changed. When he and Julian Powell-Tuck were students at the RCA they, and many others, shared a large house in Putney. Both worked with Stefanidis but as they began to receive their own small commissions they also shared a rented studio and decided to work together as Powell-Tuck and Connor. Powell-Tuck describes it as a 'mutual arrangement . . . we collaborated when the work was there . . . there was no business plan, it was basically just dealing with stuff that presented itself.'[19] That both were from Birmingham was coincidental. Powell-Tuck had trained in Brighton but they shared design principles and methodologies that had been shaped at the RCA and had art school rather than architecture school mindsets. As the workload grew they would work late with drinks and music, friends would call in, it was productive and convivial.

Occasional, more formal, studio parties were attended by the emerging leading lights in London's creative community. Surprise arrivals at one party were a short-lived artistic group calling themselves Neo-Naturalists, who included the voluptuous Leigh Bowery, and caused a stir by arriving and circulating in the nude. Neither Connor nor Powell-Tuck can remember the incident. It may be an urban myth but evidence of their significance that someone bothered to invent the story.

The architect Pierre d'Avoine, who owned the house in Putney and had met Connor when both had been undergraduates in Birmingham, shared the studio and briefly joined them as a partner. He remembers being intrigued by their collaborative brainstorming and drawing, which was a different modus operandi from the strategic analysis and rational development of ideas in plan and section that he had been taught in architecture school. Their drawings were, he says, more 'sketchy and three-dimensional'.[20] They continued to work in this collaborative way throughout their partnership. One would lead on a project and the other would act as a sounding board and critic. As the practice grew and staff multiplied, the degree of collaboration necessarily declined.

The pace of interior projects tends to be precipitous, and that of architecture protracted, and d'Avoine concluded that he needed a less frenetic working environment and moved out. Powell-Tuck and Connor made their reputation with modestly scaled interior projects but given their ambitions to deal with larger projects and architecture they thought it useful to have a professional relationship with a qualified architect. While their RCA training more than adequately equipped them to design buildings it could not grant them the formal qualifications that more cautious clients might expect. After d'Avoine left in 1982 they found their architectural partner in Gunnar Orefelt, a Swede who had studied in Stockholm and the Architectural Association in London. They became Powell-Tuck, Connor and Orefelt (P-TCO).

Connor tried to persuade Ben Kelly to join them, suggesting that the four of them could become the Beatles of interior design. Kelly preferred his independence and turned down the invitation, which, given that the Beatles had already disbanded with some rancour, was perhaps a sensible decision.

In the early 1980s it was not too far-fetched to see Connor, Powell-Tuck and Kelly as something rather like rock stars. (Kelly had just completed the Hacienda nightclub in Manchester.) They were certainly adulated by the students of interior design, and quite a few in architecture; their projects were feted in the increasing numbers of interior design magazines, for professional and popular audiences. Nick Coombe remembers that when Connor and Powell-Tuck came on stage to give a lecture about their work at the V&A museum, Connor took the microphone and said in the manner of a rock star, 'It's great to be back in the V&A.'[21] They had of course never lectured there before. It was not immodest, it was simply that he has an instinct for finding and expressing what are perhaps surreally ironical versions of the normal.

It is perhaps that appetite to amuse and that ability to relish the incongruous that shapes his work. He takes it wholly seriously but his tendency to amuse has perhaps led to his not being taken as seriously as his more pompous contemporaries.

He inclined towards a boisterous social life. At the time he chose to live in a very small flat on the King's Road a deprivation he justified by saying that he could not afford anything better or bigger in the area and preferred to live at the hub of social action rather than somewhere roomier in the suburban sticks.

Big break

Powell-Tuck and Connor made their mark with a project that was primarily Connor's. In addition to selling New Romantics their clothes, McLaren was also concocting and managing New Romantic bands of which the most successful was Adam and the Ants. The band's singer, the eponymous Adam Ant who when more prosaically named Stuart Goddard had been another resident of the Putney house, asked Connor to design his flat. This time the outcome was more Charles Dickens than Lewis Carroll. The flat looked like somewhere that the jilted Miss Havisham might have sat in her fading wedding dress doggedly waiting for the return of her absconding bridegroom. It was a stage set in which a New Romantic could perform the routines of his daily life.

Having toyed with the idea of becoming a set designer at art school, and despite three years on a quasi-architecture course at the Royal College of Art, Connor retained some instincts for the theatrical. When working with Stefanidis he had learnt some un-architectural moves and made connections that enabled him to work outside the typical territories of the RCA graduate. Fundamental to the success of the Ant flat was the faux marbling by the specialist painter David Champion. All wall and ceiling surfaces, all permanent elements, like the fireplace and door frames, were finished in marbled blue-ish, grey-ish tones. Connor made no structural alterations but fused the distinctions between rooms by having all walls and hard furniture pieces throughout the flat uniformly marbled. The diverse functions of the painted elements made their monolithic treatment all the more extraordinary.

He revealed his conceit/deceit in the small kitchen where the progressive build-up of paint layers that made up the marbling process was revealed regressively, each regression demonstrating a preparatory step in the process. The sequence ended with the flat grey base coat.

If there was any doubt about the project's evocative and provocative intent, it was

Adam Ant's flat, London: the sequential revelation of the preparatory stages of the marbling process confirm that conceit rather than deceit was the order of the day.

Adam Ant's flat, London: faux marbling, pumped-up furnishings, hard-edged geometries and extant mouldings made a compellingly ambiguous interior.

Adam Ant's flat: curtains trailed promiscuously across the floor and strategic 'measuring sticks' make it clear that provocation is intended.

dispelled by the treatment of furniture and fittings. Curtains, grey to tone with the marbling, were long enough to creep across the floor and padded, between face and lining, to bulk up and hold their folds. Winged armchairs and a sofa were over-stuffed and draped with a grey fabric specially made, with classical motifs, by Mollie Lee. An empty, marbled picture frame rested on the mantelpiece and leant on the wall for support. It was theatrical and romantic. Melancholy is romantic.

Powell-Tuck provided opinions and support but the project was essentially Connor's, which the direction of his and Powell-Tuck's subsequent work confirms. Connor did incorporate 'measuring sticks', painted poles that Powell-Tuck had evolved for an RCA projects. Horizontally striped white, red or blue, they could be rearranged for 'the creation of set pieces'.[22] They were ostensibly a strangely inappropriate addition but served to confirm that the interior was a great deal more than the conventional decoration project than a casual glance might suggest.

Powell-Tuck was working on other projects. The quality of his work was on a par with Connor's but it tended towards the rational rather than the expressionistic. His preferred materials tended to be harder, more architectonic. His first published projects – the interiors of a houseboat and a recording studio designed in collaboration with d'Avoine – had intricately painted walls by Sally Greaves-Lord but the sum of their parts was not idiosyncratic enough to cause the stir that the flats did.

Godfrey Golzen, writing in the interior supplement of the *RIBA Journal*, described the Ant flat as the new practice's 'big breakthrough' and summed it up very well as 'the faintly bizarre but arresting and influential melange of soft-edge drapery and hard-edged geometrical furniture'.[23]

Wider recognition, and occasional opprobrium, came when the *Architectural Review*, the primary design arbitrator for the architectural profession, sensed that there was something about interior design in the air and, within a year, organised two competitions for interior projects. The first was for a hypothetical jewellery shop and demonstrated the diversity of Postmodern sub-styles, from Postmodern Classicism to High Tech, that were being explored in Britain and beyond. The second was for built and unbuilt interiors. Both competitions attracted high numbers of entries, and the fact that the leading architectural magazine of record and theory was devoting 100 pages and editorial time to interior design was indicative of the way in which interiors had begun to hog the limelight. Working with interiors offered opportunities to experiment freely with the rich and varied options of the new Postmodernist orders, free from the dull necessities of making buildings secure and weather proof.

The better entries for the second competition were published in November 1982 and introduced the Ant flat to a flabbergasted audience. It was decidedly left-field and looked like it did not belong in the pages of *AR* or in any of the established architectural, design or decoration magazines. At the time it would have been difficult to explain exactly what it was about but its otherness was clear. The photographs excited young practitioners and students. They knew about Postmodernism but most were still thinking in terms of the brightly coloured caricatures of Classical models that were being cobbled together in the USA. The Ant flat was much more subtle. The judges, who were the editor of *AR* and three architectural luminaries, recognised and responded to its ambiguity. The American architect Susana Torre said it was a 'remaking of something that looks like a normal environment strangely transmuted by textual manipulation',[24] which is possibly architectural-speak for ambiguously compelling.

Connor's, and Powell-Tuck's, rationale for the project, submitted with the photographs and drawings, explained that the eccentricity of the client 'inspired a theatrical' response in which 'traditional English elements are used throughout the scheme but each element is distorted and amended to make it modern'. Significantly they did not describe it as Modernist.[25] It would have been wholly accurate to describe it as Postmodern but that would have been a foolish strategy, given the raw and unresolved prejudices surrounding that way of thinking. The concept drew on a pre-Modern domestic palette but did not flaunt extant architectural devices. Cornices, skirtings and architraves were retained but their presence was downplayed and their significance increased by the universal marbling.

The flat's success relied on its ambiguous allusions being understood subliminally rather than analytically. Powell-Tuck describes it as expressionistic and 'a little shrine' to New Romanticism.

The *AR* did not do anything as crass as declaring an outright winner in the competition and the judges' remarks hinted at their preference for a house in which occasional pieces of dark Victorian furniture were sprinkled across relentlessly white rooms. That was very much the sort of interior that the *AR* was given to publishing. It was 'architectural' and conceived by architects. It was the antithesis of the flat which offered an aggressive alternative to the cautious and well-tried good taste represented by flowing white spaces. Powell-Tuck and Connor declared that they were interested in interiors made up of autonomous rooms rather than amorphous 'spaces'.

The *AR* introduced the flat to architects and designers but, with the change in national mood that marked the transition from the apologetic 1970s to the aspirational 1980s, popular interest in interior design was blossoming amongst non-professionals and this was recognised by the publisher Kevin Kelly who launched the magazine *The World of Interiors* in 1981. The idea was initiated by Minn Hogg, a self-confessed enthusiast for 'crumbling old houses'[26] and she was its first editor. Dinah Hall, Powell-Tuck's wife and a journalist who was later to become deputy editor of *The World of Interiors*, brought the flat to Hogg's attention. The flat was Hogg's cup of tea and she put it on the magazine's cover. It had all the poignant romance that she had hitherto found in the worn fabrics, the chipped paintwork and the neglected corners of minor country houses.

The project was hugely influential but too intense and labour intensive to spawn many straight imitations. Few enthusiasts could afford the services of specialist painters to eliminate their own white walls but the idea of breaking up flat colour planes caught on. It was something that clients, unburdened by concerns about violating Modernist orthodoxies, could respond to more intuitively than could architects or Bauhausian designers.

In the same issue *AR* also published drawings for another Connor project. It was also for Adam Ant, but one that would not be built. It was to be his 'country house'. Powell-Tuck drew plans and sections and Connor provided detail and atmosphere in his characteristic perspectives. It was the first opportunity that anyone other than the few who worked in the practice had to see these extraordinary things; they had not been part of the submission for the flat. The magazine said that the project 'was thought worth a mention because of the originality of its drawings which hold promise of an apparently conventional interior strangely altered'.[27] Torre admired the project itself for the way it appeared to 'acknowledge reality in some way that is not obvious'; a perceptive description of the essential quality it shared with the flat.[28] The drawings' contorted perspectives plainly suggested German Expressionist set design and a figure that peers out from the bottom right-hand corner has a distinct resemblance to the vampire in F. W. Murnau's 1922 silent horror film *Nosferatu*.

The photographs and drawings for both projects roused the rabble, wakening something dormant in the collective imagination of interior design students and young practitioners. That something so patently outrageous had not only been conceived, but translated into a viable interior, suggested that there were strange things to be done and that the strange could become mainstream. It is intriguing to realise how modest were the means. Powell-Tuck and Connor operated frugally and were unable to afford specialist interior photographers. They took the photographs themselves and the pink

Marco Pirroni's flat, London: a sketch in which Connor reflects on, and slightly tunes, the finished room, inhabiting his most extreme interior with his most extreme representation of an 'ideal' inhabitant.

tint at the top of the curtains, in what became the most published image, was a consequence of inadequate cameras and limited technique but the accidental flash of colour confirmed that the photograph was not black-and-white and that the monotonic colour palette it captured was entirely intended.

Connor was, and remains, ambivalent about the Ant project, which he thought a little too retrospective and smacking a little of the world of Stefanidis. He may also have felt that New Romanticism lacked punk's grittiness and he remained intrigued by punk. Adam Ant's exoticism was, as Peter York has said, a bit 'panto'. Connor preferred a project that allowed him to rework, in a decidedly more anarchic fashion, the Ant elements. It was another flat for another musician, Marco Pirroni, who was then Adam Ant's lead guitarist and co-songwriter, a well-established musician with a solid punk pedigree and a habitué of McLaren's and Westwood's boutiques.

Connor's activity was confined to the most public area – the large entrance that also served as a dining area – and the other rooms were all white. As in the Ant flat, walls and furniture shared a finish but this time, in place of precisely executed marbling, they were daubed with slashes of paint, executed by Madeleine Palme, a fine artist. There was no intention that they should look like anything other than paint. Connor made his usual expressionistic/

Marco Pirroni's flat, London: a 'dog fur' chair.

Marco Pirroni's flat, London: free-form daubings on ceiling, walls and furniture offer an uninhibited counterpoint to the precise marbling in Adam Ant's flat.

impressionistic sketches and Palme worked from them. If the paint daubings were extraordinary, the physical realisations of the distorted perspectives in Connor's drawings were more so; conventional rectangular doors and frames were twisted out of shape, tops of skirtings were angled, wall-mounted radiators were hung askew. A table was pointedly triangular with a daubed paint pattern on its top, in which one might imagine one saw the Nosferatu face from the sketches. Connor specified that the retro 1950s chairs arranged around the table should be upholstered in what he called 'dog fur', which was also daubed with paint. Whether any dogs were harmed in the making of the chairs is unknown. This was a punk interior and it may be that Pirroni the former punk had been, like Connor, embarrassed to find himself transposed to the 'panto' world of New Romanticism and was keen to declare his old affinities. It would suggest that what seemed like graphic quirks were objective representations of Connor's intention.

The completion of the project in 1985 appears to have exorcised Connor's appetite for the anarchic. It may have been enough to convince clients that they did not want to follow him down that particular route. Or it may have been that, as always, he was ready to move on.

Marco Pirroni's flat, London: the two-dimensional distortion of horizontal and vertical planes makes for a room in which the calibrated stripes of the 'measuring sticks' seem rational.

California here he comes

The architectural bias of the Environmental Design course had changed the nature of Connor's experience at the RCA. He had graduated ten years before the course got its RIBA recognition but he had acquired the ambition and the ability to dabble in architecture and the opportunity to dabble came quickly.

Powell-Tuck had begun to suspect that Connor was spending too much time at the Architectural Association, where he was teaching, absorbing too much of its ethos and becoming unnecessarily interested in designing architecture. He considered that he himself remained truer to the spirit of the RCA.

Gunnar Orefelt not only provided the practice with architectural expertise, he also introduced Swedish clients, of whom the most significant was Thomas Lundstrom who, in 1982, approached the practice to design a house, which would be called Villa Zapu, on the 130 acres he had acquired in California's Napa Valley and on which he intended to plant a vineyard. The house would be secluded and isolated, set high on a ridge with views across surrounding valleys to heavily wooded hills.

Orefelt and Connor went to view the site. Orefelt decided that he would not enjoy regular commuting from London to California and left the project to Connor who realised he had been given the opportunity to design big on a big budget and was anxious not to waste it. It would be his apprentice piece but one on an enormous scale. He felt he had no excuse for failure.

He had built no exteriors in the UK nor had he made structural alterations in his interiors. If he knew little about British construction techniques he knew less about North American practices. The American way, with timber frames clad in timber boarding or panels was lighter and faster. It was also flexible and more tolerant of impulses to fine-tune and the inexperienced Connor could take advantage of this.

In the end the principles of frame construction were not difficult to understand and resolve. He had the support of local consultant architects McCracken White & Associates, who were content to find ways to make his propositions work and showed no inclination to influence their direction.

Connor began thinking about the house in his customary fashion, with a series of speculative drawings. The series of drawings for Zapu was long, very long. When it was all over, Lundstrom remembered his concern at what he felt to be the glacial development of ideas but, as the process wore on, he became aware of a steady evolution and, when construction finally finished, he realised that the configuration and proportion of elements in the completed building closely matched those in the final rounds of sketching. Coherence and continuity were evident, as each step led to the next. It was a slow process and slow progress made for tense moments, particularly when Lundstrom and his wife moved into the building before it was completed, while Connor was also in residence supervising finishing touches.

While it was possible for Connor to set down broad principles of the design in his usual sketches, the complexities of designing a large three-storey structure, perched on a hill surrounded only by trees, led him and his team in the London studio to prolific model-making. The cardboard 'sketches' that they glued together were particularly important in resolving the relationships between the setbacks and solid balustrades that shaped the top floor and the foursquare ground floor, and they provided information that he would incorporate into sketches to set up the agenda for his further exploration and the next model. The interiors were about mood and atmosphere, qualities that are best explained in drawings but a building, and particularly one to be viewed in the round, from near and far, is best viewed as an object, however scaled down.

Connor's first thoughts were not burdened with architectonic priorities. His early drawings were still concerned with atmosphere. The most eccentric were prompted by his memories of the film *Apocalypse Now*, of human skulls hanging from trees in Colonel Kurtz's jungle camp. He substituted animal skulls for human and might also have been thinking about game hung after a shoot in an English country house or of American frontiersmen's comprehensive slaughtering of local fauna. No skulls survived to the final proposal nor were they meant to; they were to get him in the mood, to flex his imagination. Nick Coombe remembers that, in the summer of 1984, as they were beginning the project, they had a studio 'outing' to two English country houses: Hawksmoor's Easton Neston and William Kent's Rousham House. Connor was looking for something that would lure him away from Modernist rationality and ensuring that his team would go with him. Villa Zapu could not be a clone of Le Corbusier's Villa Savoye.

In contrast to his gory foray into hanging skulls, his first architectonic thought was about a pair of plain square boxes, a large one for the main house and a smaller one for a guest house. He remains nostalgic for the simplicity of that diagram and wonders if he should have examined it in more detail but he sensed that such a grand project needed a more complex response than two square blocks.

It is always sensible to begin with a square. Louis Kahn recommended it and, in 1967, Michael Graves offered a two-square solution in his Hanselmann House, in which a large, much-eroded cube of the main house was joined by a bridge to the elevated, much-eroded, much-smaller cube of a guest house but it sat on a

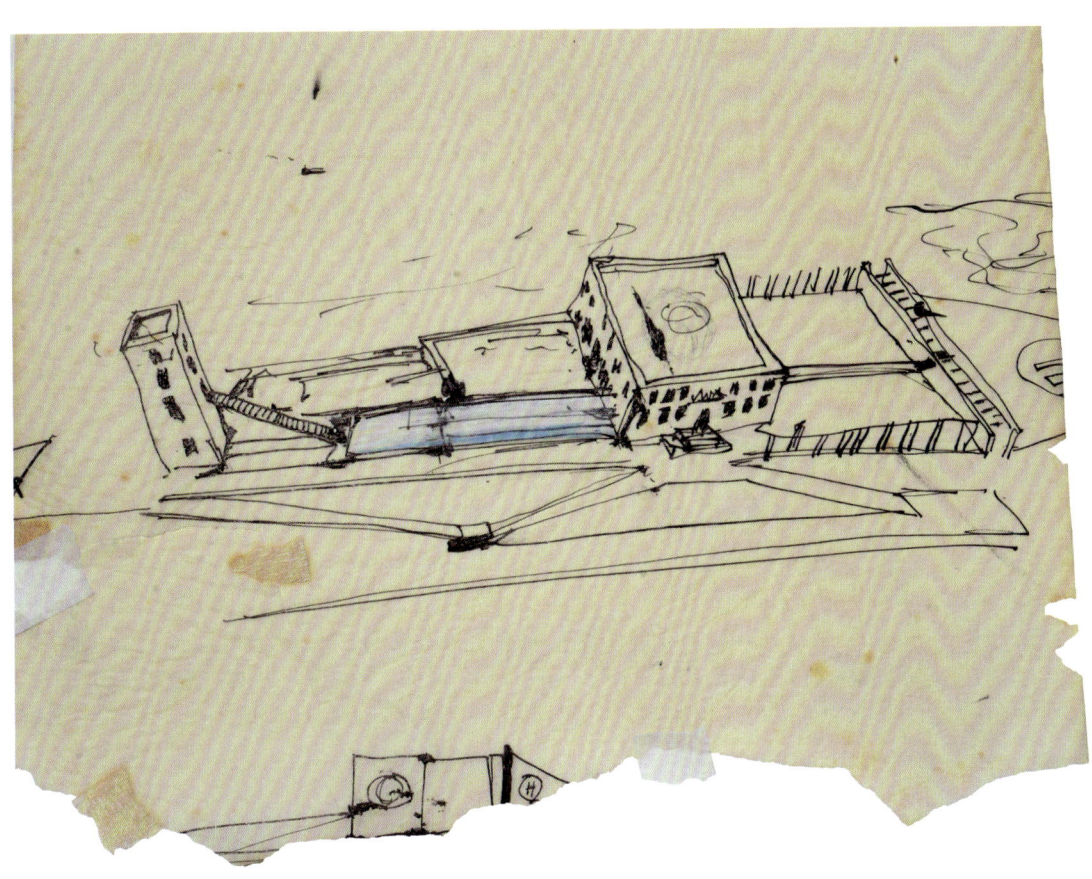

Villa Zapu, Napa, California: a speculation about two square buildings and a square entrance 'stockade'.

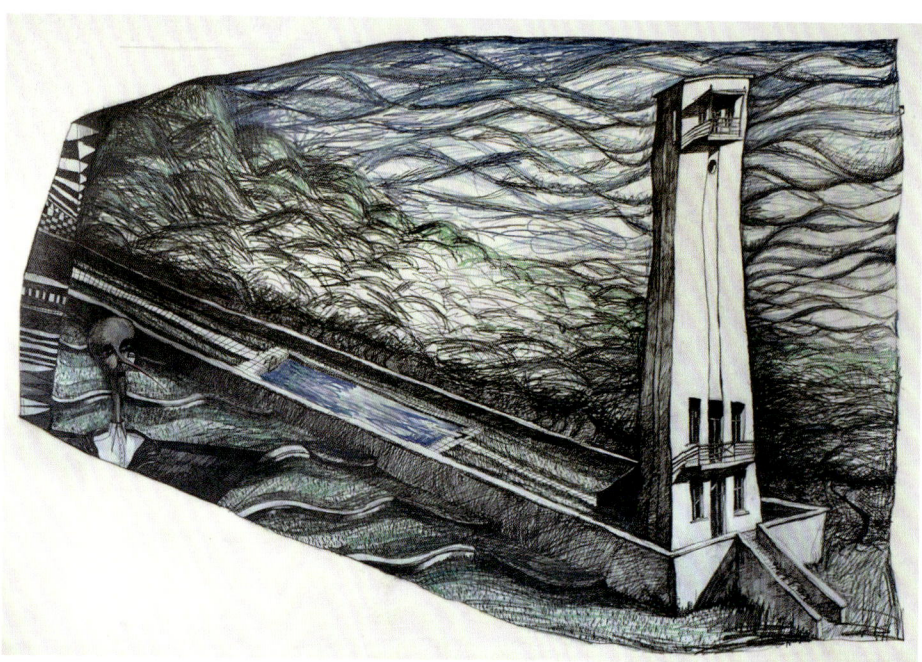

Villa Zapu, Napa, California: the entrance facade and the guest tower.

Villa Zapu, Napa, California: a model made late in the design process.

Villa Zapu, Napa, California: two views of the site, cut from the forest, with the main house stretching across its width and the tower and circular car park/helipad marking the ends of the meandering path and pool.

flat site with trees wrapped closely around it. It was Graves's deconstructing of the Modernist house in an attempt to find a richer language for domestic architecture. He would continue that search and become the most prolific exponent of colourful, cartoonish Postmodern Classicism. Zapu was not Modernist but it was very modern because it took what it needed from history. There is something oddly familiar about some of its parts.

Connor retained his two separate buildings but they no longer shared a geometry. Each became the antithesis of the other. The main house lies low and long on the crest of a hill and the guest house sits high on its own earthern plinth. They are connected, not by a bridge, but a swimming pool.

The main house is on three levels. A basement contains services, a gymnasium and a garage. The middle floor, at ground level, is a long, thin rectangle and a plinth for the upper level in which walls are set back to make strips and wedges of balconies. On its narrow ends the principal rooms of the upper floor are cantilevered far beyond the lower, the acutely angled projection to the east contains the master bedroom and that to the west is a square block containing a guest bedroom. The ground falls steeply away below the master bedroom's cantilever and its angle is replicated in the external stair that sits beside it and leads to the ground level terrace. The sharply-angled cantilevers hang like shards left after the missing end of the building had slithered down the hill.

The horizontal banding of the long elevations could be seen as Modernist but its secondary elements contradict that. The interiors of the ground-floor public rooms are linked, visually and physically, to the landscape by high floor-to-ceiling windows and they, like the windows on the upper floor, are cut into thick solid walls. They are not horizontal Modernist strips of glass walls. Only the windows in the two cantilevered ends of the upper floor have a horizontal bias and offer no support to the solid walls above them, suggesting that they are the precarious remnants of a crumbling structure.

The horizontality of the long elevations is bisected by vertical elements that mark primary entrance points. Something about the angled edge of that to the south suggests a pylon at the entrance to an Egyptian temple. It is the arrival point for visitors who have walked from a parking area lower down the hill and it fronts a small enclosed area, a sort of pedestrianised *porte-cochère* off which tall doors lead to the double height hall. On the opposite side a second straight-edged structure projects above the roof line and leads to the terrace and a flight of steps to the pool and the guest tower beyond. Its verticality connects it to the tower.

Zapu was designed at a time when, following the Postmodernist purge of Modernism's dogma, Classical planning principles were intriguing architects and encouraging the reintroduction of more formal interactions of interior spaces. Zapu's corridors are dramatised by forced perspectives, and movement from the entrance hall to principal public rooms is punctuated by pairs of double doors that lead to and from lofty anterooms. The double height entrance area sets out to match the grandeur of the formal entrance halls in Neoclassical country houses but is without the benefits of Neoclassical ornamental devices. The stair that would have stood foursquare and airy as the centrepiece of the room is pushed into a corner and enclosed by walls that are twisted off the square and the vertical. Of all the elements of the building the entrance space comes closest to being Modernist and its success depends on the manipulation of plain planes. It was in this manipulation that the versatility of timber frame construction paid off. The complex three-dimensionality was impossible to draw by hand or the computer softwares of the time but on-site Connor and the carpenters sketched out options with lengths of timber.

A narrow external stair at right angles to the building connects the upper floor to the external terrace that runs the length of the ground floor and the shorter, wider flight of steps leading to the swimming pool that sits between the house and the guest tower. Connor's first thought was that guests would be obliged to swim to the tower. Whatever stress the project may have put him under it seems not to have curbed his wayward impulses. In the end this obligation was relaxed and guests were permitted to walk along the broad edges of the pool.

The straight flight of external stairs to the first floor and the pool share an axis with a third narrow external stair that climbs to the entrance door for the tall tower that is the guesthouse. In the spirit of equality, two visitor suites sit above and two below the entrance level, to minimise the chore of guests having to climb up, or down, to their rooms. The elevation that looks away from the house over miles of raw country is less solid, with floor-to-ceiling windows and balconies for long views across the surrounding heavily wooded, steep-sided valleys and hills.

The height of the tower is increased by the circular terraced plinth on which it sits. It suggests something medieval, perhaps conjured up from memories of the books and pictures that had amused the infant Connor. If the main building suggests a Neoclassical country house, the tower is a medieval castle sitting on its motte. The narrow external entrance stairs also suggest a strategy for repelling attackers as boiling oil could be conveniently pored from the small square windows directly above the door. The impression of medievalism is underlined by long thin 'heraldic' flags hung from poles that project from either side of the top floor and drop to ground level. It is a folly and, as a good folly should, enhances the landscape in which it sits.

Villa Zapu, Napa, California: the path from the car park snakes, like the swathes of grasses, to the entrance pylon.

A drawing of the tower, complete with its banners, appeared on the vineyard's bottle labels, like the drawings of chateaux on the bottles of the better Bordeaux wines.

Both Zapu buildings displayed a Postmodernist willingness to learn from history but whereas American exponents of that tendency favoured literal and colourful reworkings of historical motifs, Connor drew on precedent more eclectically and avoided cartoonish pastiche. He understood how to iron out his more extreme initial indulgences to produce bona fide architecture.

Zapu's interiors are formally glamorous and the white walls, within and without, recognise the impact of Californian sunlight and that much of Californian indoor life melds with the outdoor. Connor now thinks that his presumptions about the Californian climate were simplistic and, later, when he lived in the South of France, he realised that allowing winter sun to penetrate interiors is as important as keeping summer sun at bay.

In *Roughing It,* an account published in 1872 of his time spent in California, Mark Twain suggested that the state's scenery was best enjoyed from a distance, arguing that the limited variety and scale of its vegetation became monotonous at close range. Zapu's relationship to the landscape suggests that Connor had arrived, after a less immersive experience, at a similar conclusion. The house and tower were well placed to offer long views of wooded hills but he was left with the problem of how to integrate them into their more immediate surroundings. He took comfort and confidence from having written, in a dissertation at the RCA, about 18th-century English landscaping principles for placing a large house in stage-managed parkland. He did not suppose that the villa would be surrounded by parterres or an English country garden and evolved something that was closer in spirit to the rolling parklands of William Kent or Capability Brown.

The design process is serendipitous; possibilities are suggested at random and a well-tuned imagination can spot potential in odd places. When making a perspective drawing of the long elevation of the house, Connor found himself with a large expanse of empty white foreground and spontaneously filled it with serpentine ribbons of different textures and tones, perhaps prompted by thoughts of contour lines or terraced vineyards. It occurred to him that these could be realised as swathes of different grasses. Hargreaves Associates, then an emerging team of landscaping consultants, translated the diagram into viable reality. They identified and mapped out bands of different grasses, some to grow long and course, some short and fine, to provide tones and textures that would accentuate the contours of the site. The bands gave a casual formality to the immediate surroundings of

Villa Zapu, Napa, California: the shard of the principal bedroom hangs over the eastern edge of the site.

Villa Zapu, Napa, California: the house and pool from the tower.

Villa Zapu, Napa, California: the tower with wafting banners (wafting curtains are a recurring phenomenon in Connor's interior drawings).

Villa Zapu, Napa, California: the verticality of the tower is echoed in the portico of the main house.

Villa Zapu, Napa, California: the stair well and high entrance hall veer unexpectedly from the orthogonal geometries of the rest of the house.

Graphic studio, Los Angeles: as drawn.

Above: Napa Creek apartments, California: the low relief modelling of the facade demonstrates that Connor was finding decorative potential in the mechanics of North American timber frame construction.

Top and above: Graphic studio, Los Angeles: as built.

the house and tower – enough to confirm that things were not entirely natural. Vertical metal strips between different grasses ensured that the designated shapes of strips were not lost in the mowing process. The strategy was close in spirit to the naturalistic herbaceous planting principles that Piet Oudolf was evolving in the Netherlands around the same time.

Zapu was not Connor's only Californian building. Though his unfamiliarity with American building practice would have led some builders to question his ability, his willingness to acknowledge and exaggerate his innocence was disarming to Zapu's broad-minded builder. He was a Harvard MBA with ambitions beyond contracting and was on the point of developing a small apartment block in the city of Napa. He recognised that Connor could produce an attention-grabbing building and asked him to design the block. Connor was not wholly satisfied with the result but the options for stacking identical units one above the other are few and, compared to the possibilities offered by Zapu, the modest block was inevitably going to be an anti-climax for him. Whatever he thought of them, the apartments were let quickly and at a premium price.

He was happier with another little building he designed in Los Angeles. The client was a graphic designer whom Powell-Tuck had known at Brighton. Powell-Tuck was involved in the design but it was logical that Connor should take over the project since he was commuting from London at least once a month. (He now thinks he should have visited the Zapu site more frequently but as a young and, he thought, unproven designer he was chary of spending his client's money too freely.) The studio was a small, very cheap but elegantly jaunty building perched on top of a rough and ready garage. It is easy to see in it hints of Zapu, particularly the small square, regularly spaced windows and the tall glazed facade that stretches above the roofline of the rest of the building.

Connor considered moving to California. He knew from the better examples of bigger buildings that were appearing that interesting possibilities existed but he was worried about how long it would take him to attract that scale of work. Nor was he sure that he wanted it; he was not inclined to set up the professional organisation necessary to deal with substantial projects and he disliked the impact that cars and parking lots had on the way buildings were used. He had a European taste for street life. He, or rather P-TCO could have, legally, opened a second office in the USA but his accountant warned him that it would be potentially dangerous to distance himself from developments in London.

And at the most fundamental level he was not sure he wanted to adjust to life in California; he had begun to find the climate too predictably pleasant and, in the end, it seemed that more interesting things were happening in London. But, with Zapu, he left behind a serious piece of architecture and, as Powell-Tuck said, 'Zapu was David's baby completely'.[29]

The end of the beginning

Despite a certain paucity of architectural qualifications it could be convincingly argued that P-TCO were the most exciting young architectural practice of the 1980s. They certainly won the support of journalists. A profile of the practice in the *RIBA Journal* of December 1985 by Godfrey Glozen was titled 'Doing What Architects Used To Do'. The phrase was borrowed from a statement by Powell-Tuck in which he said, 'We always try to persuade our clients to let us design everything – the interior (he had his unofficial architect's hat on), the furniture, even the rugs on the floor. In fact we do what architects used to do up until the 1940s.'[30] He regretted that 'good architecture is a labour of love. In other words it's uneconomic on its own.'[31] Accordingly the partnership developed other income-generating activities. Powell-Tuck was already designing furniture and lighting and the practice had opened a cafe near their studio, an oddly entrepreneurial thing to do in the early 1980s. It did not last long. They did not have time to develop it and they had no ambitions to become caterers.

In the 1970s, Britain's shaky economy and the paralysing confrontations between governments and strike-happy trade unions led to its becoming the latest in a line of malfunctioning countries to be declared the sick man of Europe. That changed abruptly, and unexpectedly, after the Thatcher government negotiated the deregulation of financial markets. The Stock Exchange accepted electronic trading and shed its traditional ponderous way of operating. Membership of the Exchange was opened to foreign banks and bankers poured in. The lifestyle of stock market traders became part of 1980s mythology. Very quickly a great many made a great deal of money and competed to spend it recklessly and ostentatiously in restaurants and on lavishly decorated homes. Other wealthy foreigners began to see the country as a desirable and secure place in which to live and invest. Amongst them were a sizeable number of Swedes, and Orefelt knew many of them. The practice began to specialise in Swedish clients.

Property speculation was in the air and new buildings transfigured by Postmodernist detailing were insinuating themselves into public consciousness. Architecture was becoming popular and even banks were keen to invest in design-related opportunities. Commercial interior design companies were floating on the stock exchange and while their founders became surprisingly rich (one collected £53 million in the mid-1980s) the creative energy that had made them big was dissipated and sidelined as shareholders' dividends became paramount. Expedient creativity did help to keep profits high. Powell-Tuck, Connor and Orefelt were not inclined to hand over creative control to shareholders but they did see interesting possibilities in property development, which was an ambition in tune with the spirit of the entrepreneurial 1980s that gave them, barring brush-ins with planning authorities, complete creative freedom. Orefelt used his contacts with potential Swedish clients to raise capital. The practice's strategy was to find what they called 'back land' sites – abandoned or neglected spaces set behind terraces of houses and shops and which were typically devoted to light-industrial activities but could be transformed into enclaves that had a rakish glamour.

Their first venture was small. In south-west London they found a 'back land' site for which they persuaded planners to give permission for a single house. To their surprise their bank, which was presumably aware of the practice's successes and might have hoped for a little glamour by association, gave them all the money they needed to match that put up by the project's builder. Powell-Tuck was primarily responsible for a very pretty little white-rendered house. It had deep-set square windows that allowed sunlight to dapple its internal walls.

It had a projecting entrance portico/pylon that looked very like a miniaturised version of the entrance to Zapu. The house sold quickly to one of Orefelt's Swedes and the partners were surprised to discover that they had made a substantial profit, which they decided to invest in their next speculation.

Their success increased their confidence and ambition and projects became bigger and more commercial. They found another 'back land' site in a Kensington mews and built a two-storey office block, which was primarily designed by Orefelt. They split the building vertically, moved into one half and sold the other to a Swedish ship broker. This became a formula: they would relocate the practice into the new block and sell its predecessor to raise money to pay off their loan.

They were evolving a new template for how they might function. They aimed to keep the design practice independent, separate from property development. Profits would allow them to take on and devote extra studio time to the more interesting projects, which would be required to do no more than break even. Old school developers continued to be cautious about radical design but financial autonomy allowed P-TCO the freedom to push the design of their developments further at a time when potential tenants were increasingly keen to inhabit more stimulating buildings. Of the partners, Orefelt was most interested in and

Hyde Park penthouses, London: the drawing shows increasing awareness of, and appetite for, architectural detail.

Hyde Park penthouses, London: an interior of Hogarthian decadence (the title of the drawing is incorporated in the resolutely un-rectangular border).

adept at property speculation and, as their involvement grew, they brought in a financial manager, Guy Leech, to support him.

Connor's involvement in development activities was light and in 1985 he was concentrating on a large commissioned project for two penthouse flats, overlooking Hyde Park: it would be built across the roofs of two mansion block flats bought by Swedish clients. He produced a solution that showed an affinity to, but a clear evolution from, his little flats for Ant and Pirroni. It prompted some of his most evocative drawings, perspective sketches of a complex roofscape of lead-clad mansards and grand interiors with billowing curtains, filled with his familiar cast of elegant degenerates. The drawing was as vigorous as ever but made with greater precision. Experience of completing buildings had increased his understanding of detail and that awareness was enriching the drawings. The more careful delineation of elements made them the more remarkable but tipped chairs and spilt wine provided undeniable evidence of debauchery. He enjoyed the process so much that he created drawn frames.

He was also spending time in the Far East. British interior design was being extensively featured in Asian magazines and P-TCO were approached by Pinhole, a Taiwanese company that offered a design and build service. Pinhole's principals had seen photographs of the musicians' flats and decided that something similar would do very well for their customers. Connor produced proposals and an experienced assistant, Mark Lintott, was dispatched to Taiwan to liaise and develop ideas. The number of Taiwanese projects increased rapidly and soon other assistants were relocated to join him. Connor was also a regular visitor and enjoyed the social life – and the creative opportunities. Projects, principally nightclubs and restaurants, were designed and built very quickly and established P-TCO's reputation. They were also asked to design a number of private houses and Connor enjoyed getting to grips with local idiosyncrasies. One worldly owner requested that there should be accommodation on his roof for two monks, who would act as his proxies and devote themselves to compensating for his spiritual shortcomings. There were interesting cultural misalignments. Connor and Lintott collaborated on an Italian restaurant on Taipei's main street and became involved in discussions about an appropriate name for it. Connor offered Mussolini as a facetious option and the clients, unfamiliar with, or unperturbed by, details of European history, preferred it to their own suggestions. He persuaded them to settle for M Café.

Increasing workloads and more complex projects meant that Connor and Powell-Tuck were collaborating less in the early stages of each other's projects. That changed when a

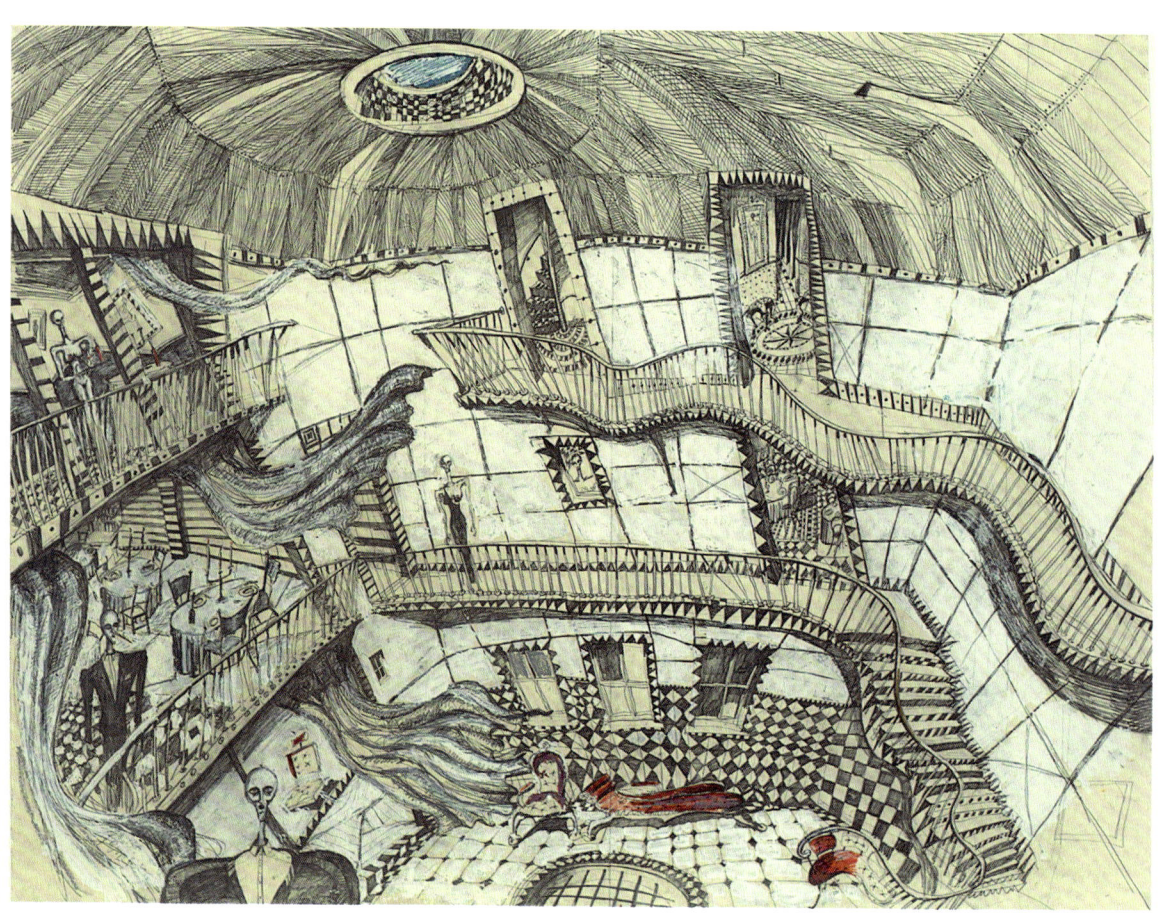

Roppongi nightclub, Tokyo: much of the project's detail evolved in the making of this sketch.

client Powell-Tuck had cultivated in Japan asked them to design a bar and club in Tokyo. At the time Tokyo was the most expensive city in the world and, just as the rigour of Japanese design was admired by designers in the West, Japanese hospitality entrepreneurs, and their fashion-conscious customers, were enthusiastic about British design, which delivered a more diverse and indulgent aesthetic. The site was in Roppongi, a district of bars and clubs in the centre of Tokyo. Powell-Tuck developed a strategy for the building and asked Connor to make sketches of the interior, which established the detailing strategy. Both were excited about the project and the future work it would attract in Japan, but in 1989 a collapse of the Japanese economy began 20 years of economic stagnation and the project was never evolved or built and no others followed.

In Britain the size of projects undertaken by the practice's development wing grew steadily and in 1987 they embarked on Alice Court, a development that consumed the better part of a street in Putney. They had backing from Saudi Arabian investors who were also beginning to see the potential of the London property market. The development took four years from the acquisition of the site to completion and it was unfortunately timed. 1989 also saw the beginning of economic recession in Britain and a precipitous drop in property values. The market value of new buildings became significantly less than the money owed to pay for their construction. P-TCO came close to salvaging the deal with a sale to a Swedish pension fund but not quite quickly enough. They were not bankrupt but lost all the money they had made. They could no longer afford to run the design practice which had grown and now employed 20 assistants. The partners decided that they had to break it up and did so. Connor remembers with gratitude and affection how, as they sat on a bench in their local park, Powell-Tuck suggested that while they had lost their money they should not lose their friendship. They have not done so. The end of the partnership was the result of economic circumstances that destroyed most of the big and not so big interior design studios that had over-expanded in the heady days of the decade of design.

Connor had not been very interested in, or suited to, negotiating loans and keeping his eye on real estate fluctuations. He had been a happy beneficiary, at least on paper, of the period of prosperity that followed their speculations but had begun to feel increasingly uneasy about his role in the partnership. He remembers arriving at the studio one morning to find the courtyard unusually full of 'black cars' and finding 'men in black suits' gathered round the meeting room table.[32] He realised that he had little to offer at such existential meetings, that he would understand very little of what was being discussed and was not very

Apartment block, Taiwan: Connor finds what variations he can on the theme of stacked flats and adds a little romance as one of his evening-dressed men on the street serenades an evening-dressed woman on the fourth floor.

interested in finding out. He was also conscious that Powell-Tuck and Orefelt were bringing in much more work than he. Powell-Tuck had also begun designing what was to become one of the most acclaimed interior projects of the 1990s: Metropolis, his spectacular conversion of an Edwardian bus depot to a recording studio. If Connor had produced the projects that had established the practice's profile in the 1980s it was likely that, had the practice continued, Metropolis would have defined it in the 1990s. After the recession clients became cautious and more corporate, and while Metropolis was an aesthetic triumph it also demonstrated Powell-Tuck's ability to deal with technological challenges. There were very few iconoclasts amongst the new breed of clients.

From their beginning Connor recognised that Powell-Tuck had a clearer vision of how the practice might grow and how it should be organised to attract corporate clients and bigger, more commercial projects. He recognises that he has always been inclined to become too involved with the project in hand to think about a bigger picture.

Whether two designers as temperamentally and stylistically unalike as Connor and Powell-Tuck would have held together as the functioning and creative partnership that had begun 15 years earlier when they met at the RCA, is questionable. Connor's strength was for singular, quirky projects but his clients, the contrarians who had shaped the music and fashion industries in the 1980s, were being subsumed or displaced by corporate entities with layers of decision-makers and strategies thrashed out in board rooms. Such corporate functionaries were building on the foundations established by the radicals but they were not impressed by lone operators who appeared to be enjoying their work too much.

Connor found the split difficult. He no longer felt 'rich and successful', realised that he had to start again and retreated to work on his own in another small rented office.[33] He began to slip below the radar, principally due to the disappearance, in the same financial crisis that sundered the old firm, of the specialist interior magazines that would have continued to publish his work.

His reputation gave him some momentum but he admits that he was neither equipped for nor, more importantly, interested in working for big companies. He became David Connor Design and described the practice thus: 'We design interiors, new buildings and remodel old buildings'.[34] But no opportunities on a par with Zapu came his way; commercial developers wanted commercial architects. As the 1990s recovered from recession, the scale of commercial development in London was cranking up. Architectural practices were getting bigger and multi-disciplinary, and dealing with increasingly complex and streamlined construction techniques. In a market saturated with architects who were short of work he was too small to compete, even at a starter level, and continued to deal primarily with interiors.

With the end of P-TCO the partners decided to hand the Taiwan studio over to Lintott. Connor continued to work with him at the conceptual stage of a number of projects but his own workload, as a sole practitioner with occasional support, made it difficult for him to make the Taiwan commute, which may have been unfortunate, for the Far Eastern market continued to employ British designers and Mark Lintott Design remains a successful interior practice that has expanded its operations into China and Japan. Connor however enjoyed London too much to make a permanent move.

the middle

A foreign field

In the last year of P-TCO Connor had begun working on a project that was better suited to his strengths and inclinations. In 1992, The Universal Exposition of Seville (Expo '92) was organised to celebrate the 500th anniversary of Columbus's setting sail from the city on his way to 'discovering' the Americas. Even by the standards of international expos it was a major event, with a site that occupied 215 hectares. More than 100 countries took part and over six months it had 42 million visitors.

There was an official British pavilion which was big – 7000 sq m – and in the manner of its creators, Grimshaw Architects, was distinctly high-tech, with the obligatory 'kit-of-parts' made up of a prefabricated white tubular steel structure that supported glass cladding panels and lightweight screens that blocked the sun. A 65-m-long cascade of water cooled its entrance facade and doubled as a 'visitor experience'.

A glass box was a perverse response to dealing with the extreme heat of the Andalucian summer but, in a time before concerns about climate change dominated design agendas, such problems could be solved with energy-guzzling technologies. And a glass wall with a cooling waterfall was the kind of thing expected of an expo exhibit. Other pavilions were spread thickly over the rest of the site and all did their best to look modern and suggest that they, their contents and their country belonged to 1992 rather than 1592. There was one exception, a building that would not have looked modern even in 1592.

Britain's Department of Trade and Industry commissioned the Grimshaw pavilion to display the country's industrial and technological achievements but, in the name of soft power, they also commissioned a more modest proposal to promote Britain as a place of radical creativity and they asked Anish Kapoor, who was beginning to make his reputation as a sculptor and maker of conceptual installations, to provide the exhibit. He asked Connor to collaborate.

Connor and Kapoor were old friends. Their paths had first crossed in the 1970s when

Building for a Void, Seville: the tower is free of stylistic devices that would place it definitively in past, present or future.

Connor was at the RCA and Kapoor was a post-graduate student at Chelsea School of Art. Each was to be best man at the other's wedding and the two could be mutually supportive in other ways. Connor had been asked to commission bespoke works of art for Villa Zapu. Nick Coombe remembers that when working on the ground-floor plan, with its long tapering corridor, Connor proclaimed that the corridor should end with 'Anish' (a pun on 'a niche').[35] His mind works in mysterious ways.

Connor and Kapoor sat on the roof of Connor's flat and made some sketches. Connor proposed a circular tower and Kapoor an apparently bottomless pit within it, an illusion to infinite space. He proposed to achieve this by having visitors look into the very dark blue interior of a sphere buried below ground level. The sphere was Kapoor's idea and, perhaps with the guest tower for Zapu still occupying his imagination, Connor suggested a tower, a 15-m-high tapering cylinder, to contain it. Kapoor suggested that the original circular plan could be elliptical, which Connor was happy to accept. Visitors would climb to a door just under half way up its height by a steep and narrow ramp that wound itself around the outside of the cylinder and looked like the thread of a huge screw, suggesting that the tower was being screwed into, or unscrewed from, the earth.

There was logic in obliging visitors to make the climb. Towers are intrinsically interesting and this one, with a narrow little door and no windows, gave no clues to its function. It was ambiguous enough to encourage those visitors willing to sample something other than the modernistic trade pavilions to climb the ramp. And the act of climbing was disorientating; the curious were climbing to a limbo and the experience they were offered was not quite earth-bound. Some visitors, not concerned with Kapoor's profundities, might have seen it all as a metaphor for Columbus's voyage, with the ramp as the journey of discovery that allowed one to travel to and look into the unknown. At the top of the ramp visitors passed through the narrow door and entered the cylinder's dark interior. The room appeared to have been delicately excavated from the tower's solid core. It retained the elliptical plan but its walls and ceiling were fused to become a half ovoid. In the centre of the room, at the apex of the ovoid, a small oculus let in a little light that was concentrated into an intense spot that moved around the edge of the floor as the sun moved around the sky, but the focus of the room was on another little hole in the centre of the floor, the void in the ovoid. Those peering into it could imagine they were looking into a bottomless pit. Construction details added to that illusion; the edge of the hole was angled sharply back so that, when peering into the darkness one was not aware

Building for a Void, Seville: a sharp-edged ellipse of sunlight moves around the interior as the Andalucian sun moves across the sky.

Building for a Void, Seville: the dark 'bottomless' pit in the centre, the bright narrow doorway and the ellipse of sunlight.

of any substantial structure beneath one. The floor seemed dangerously fragile and the drop did appear to be of infinite depth. The illusion had artistic intent: it was profound for those who chose to look for that, but theatrical and entertaining for the casual expo-goer.

The concept was clear but difficult to build, and costly. The Spanish Government's practice of waiting 90 days before paying bills caused frustration for the British builders and concern for the British designers anxious not to miss an inflexible opening date. The eventual structural solution, devised by a British engineer, was necessarily complicated. The tower looked heavy and very solid and the first suggestion was that it should be constructed of concrete poured *in situ*; but to do that would have been time-consuming, as building a mould into which the concrete would be poured was made complex by the tower's tapering profile and the concrete would require time to set before further work could follow on. A hybrid frame of steel and timber was substituted, to be covered in mesh and rendered outside and plastered within. The earthy colour of the render suggested sun-dried mud and the building looked like it belonged in Andalucia. The interior was finished with smooth polished plaster, which made the perfect single concave plane that fused wall and ceiling. The curved surfaces made both rendering and plastering challenging for the British tradesmen who had been attracted by the opportunity to spend time working in southern Spanish sunshine. Connor and Kapoor visited every month and 'hung out'. It was an antidote to Britain in a recession.

The void itself was mysterious but achieved prosaically. It was a standard fibreglass spherical storage unit of a type used locally in the production of olive oil. Its inside was transformed with a thick coat of navy blue pigment to give a matt light-deadening finish applied by what Connor describes as a 'flocking' process. Those curious visitors who wanted to investigate further could reach into it and would later be identified as they walked through the park by the blue pigment that was transferred from their fingers to their face.

After completion Kapoor felt that the hole was not big enough but there had been no time to test prototypes and a hole that was too big might have revealed too much about the true nature and dimensions of the orifice. Size was perhaps not that important. There was wonder, sharpened by vertigo, for visitors who stood on the edge of a palpable hole and stared into what appeared to be an infinite space. It was art but had enough of the funfair about it to hold its own amongst the commercial pavilions. (The similarity of the tower to a helter-skelter could not be ignored.)

As artists are prone to do, Kapoor continued to make versions of the void. If the Seville tower might have been described as an ascent to limbo, his second iteration, also completed in 1992, was titled *Descent into Limbo* and displayed at the Documenta exhibition in Kassel in Germany. It had a larger hole placed inside a more modest structure, a concrete cube which was entered at ground level through another narrow door. This was a temporary exhibit and did not warrant the construction of a second tower but Connor made technical drawings for the blockwork construction that was finished with a smooth render to passably imitate concrete. He also made sketches, to satisfy his own curiosity: he was not quite ready to give up thinking about an empty room. (Kapoor later obtained exclusive use of a black paint, developed for military use, which absorbed 99.96 per cent of light and made the illusion of infinity both more complete and more disconcerting; Seville's blue was by comparison an amiable colour. He continued to produce versions of the void and in 2016 in Portugal a visitor fell into an even bigger hole, three metres in diameter. Any initial fright that he might have experienced on tumbling into what purported to be the infinity of a black hole was soon ended when he hit the bottom a measly two and a half metres below.)

Extravaganzas such as expos are notoriously expensive and do not pay for themselves in an accountable form. It is assumed that benefits are reaped in goodwill and ancillary trade and there were other site-specific artworks on the Seville site collectively signalling the virtues of their sponsors. The standard justification for these unquantifiables was delivered: the exhibits would be retained and maintained for the benefit of locals and those tourists searching for some relief from the relentlessly historic city. The exhibition site was scheduled to become a public park but responsibility for developing and maintaining it was passed between local and national authorities and there was no more popular enthusiasm for modern art amongst the citizens of Seville than there would have been in any other city – and even less amongst tourists who came to enjoy its glamorous past. Of all the exhibits perhaps only the tower had the picturesque timelessness that might have appealed to either group but its survival was not left to popular opinion. Various, more vulnerable, pieces of art were vandalised and the tower was smeared with graffiti. A more popular plan was concocted to make the expo site an amusement park and the developers decided that, however glaringly obvious its resemblance to a helter-skelter, the tower was on the site of their 'rapid river ride' and demolished it.

In a BBC News programme in 2010 about the destruction of the art installations, Connor declared the purging 'a colossal waste' and, while regretting the loss of all the pieces of art, a local critic, Juan Bosco Díaz Urmeneta singled out the tower: 'It was a place of calm. Amid the noise and festivity of the (expo) fair, it was like a monastery.'[36] Which was not the kind of building that would be welcome in a funfair.

Connor made two very large drawings of the tower. In one, 2.2 m high and 1.2 m wide, it was shown against an agitated sky. In the other, 2.2 m long and 1.2 m high, a structure, closely resembling the tower, was shown in the distance, isolated on a spit of land that bisected the drawing. It and the glowering sky behind it were mirrored in a watery foreground. These images suggest that the towers of Zapu and Seville were occupying a place in his imagination while he tried to concentrate on more mundane projects. He kept the first drawing but regrets selling the second, perhaps inevitably, to a Swede.

Re-starts

Connor's first sizeable project after the breakup of P-TCO was for the transformation of an inter-war ballroom in the basement of the 1930s Regent Palace Hotel, off Piccadilly, London, into something better suited to the 1990s. Oliver Peyton, born on Ireland's Atlantic coast, asked him to design what became the Atlantic Bar and Grill. Peyton had progressed from setting up successful nightclubs in the early 1980s and, as someone on the periphery of the music industry, knew about Connor's work and realised he was a man with whom he could do profitable business. He understood that 'restaurants should be about having fun' and that one did not go to a restaurant because one was hungry.[37]

Peyton was an independent operator and prepared to run risks. He had taken out a short lease – Connor remembers it as two years – which had to include the fit-out. The business had to make money quickly. Design and build were completed in three months and the two processes necessarily overlapped. Helped by two freshly graduated students, Connor speedily evolved a broad concept that established the planning strategy and an economic palette of materials. Detailed decisions were made just ahead of the construction programme, which was carried out by a shop-fitter friend of Peyton's. The three months of construction were tense. Connor thought Peyton 'pushy but fun'.[38] He was impressed by his skill and determination in establishing the formula for a successful restaurant: getting the ambience right, getting the quality of food right and getting the right clientele, who would spend money and bring with them credibility and glamour. Peyton also ensured success by somehow acquiring a licence that allowed him to sell alcohol until 3am at a time when bars were obliged to close at 11pm. The late licence and the surviving elements of the original building, tuned up by Connor, suggested something of a speakeasy and helped the Atlantic to flourish for ten years.

Atlantic Bar and Grill, London: the visual extravagance of exhumed decoration, and a tight budget, prompted atypical restraint. The barstools and ruched bases of the tub chairs had just enough of Art Deco about them to sit comfortably with the original elements.

The resuscitation of the shabby old shell began with the stripping out of plasterboard partitions and these were found to have been hiding original Art Deco elements that had presumably been incarcerated because they were deemed unacceptably old-fashioned at some point in the previous 60 years. They were a welcome find for Peyton who found he had acquired a full-blooded period piece. Sixty years seems to be about the time that needs to lapse before a disregarded style is rehabilitated in popular taste but Art Deco was the single reworking of Modernist principles, albeit one prone to pastel ornamental excesses, that found and never lost popular favour.

The reclamation reduced Connor's time-poor workload and it also gave him reference points for the elements he added – a new entrance area, a new bar and new lighting. His colours and bespoke furniture broadly took their cues from the extant Deco-isms and confirmed that the Atlantic was somewhere new and not a quaint survivor. He was relieved when the cheap velour fabric, dictated by the sparse budget, that covered the seating in his booths and looked garish in the empty space turned out to be just fine when the room was filled with customers – and it was consistently very well filled. The resuscitated room quickly became extremely fashionable. After an opening night when very few turned up, the second night was packed and, Connor was pleased to see, with the right kind of people, not just those who would appreciate his efforts but those whose attendance would open the floodgates to a tsunami of fashionistas and the hobbledehoy who would follow them.

The Atlantic was a departure from his previous work in that he was working with and taking cues from an existing interior. Without the constraints of time and budget it is impossible to say whether a comprehensive Connor makeover would have been even more successful. His previous projects had offered him blank canvases and he might not have taken on such a circumscribed brief had he had comparable opportunities elsewhere but it did offer him a way into the British market for bars and restaurants which, as the 1990s wore on, was to become increasingly important.

Another opportunity to move into what became the 'hospitality sector' loomed. Two members of the Irish band U2 had decided to convert the Clarence, a neglected Edwardian hotel on the bank of Dublin's River Liffey, into something more suitable for the tourist-centric Temple Bar area, and asked a number of practices for their ideas. It was an investment with sentimental undertones – the Clarence had been the only bar that would serve them when they were scruffy youths. Connor made a four-hour presentation to Bono and The Edge. He had employed a few assistants to work on the presentation materials and the office

Vivienne Westwood, Davies Street, London: clothes and interior shared visual references and decorative imagery recreated by newly-arrived digital printing techniques.

appeared to be bustling, and he thought he had been most persuasive. He was surprised when the commission went to established specialists in hotel design. He thinks his studio, even with its inflated numbers, may have seemed to be too small to deal with a project on that scale. Or it may have been that when the excitement generated by the presentation had time to die down the musicians decided that Connor's idea of what a hotel should be would be an investment risk too far.

Chain gang (1)

After an acrimonious split from Malcolm McLaren, Vivienne Westwood had succeeded in establishing herself as a major couture brand and, in 1992, asked Connor to design the interior of her new shop in the most fashionable shopping street in Mayfair. It was geographically some considerable distance from the wrong end of the King's Road in Chelsea and even further in terms of the expectations of her new couture customers.

It was a happy reunion. Both had matured and found their own voices since they had first met. She was 'nice to work with' and he was happy to 'hang on' as, unlike the opinionated and dogmatic McLaren, she tended to make oblique allusions to how she would like the shop to look and left it to him to give that its form.[39]

He considered collaboration with her to be 'worthwhile' and the fact that he could not easily second guess her wishes stimulating.

When he began work she was thinking about her next collection and had been hunting in the archives of the Courtauld Institute of Art to find inspiration for the printed fabrics. She had been drawn to images of 18th-century Baroque interiors but she was also using contemporary, abstracted, close-up photographs of tresses of long blonde hair.

Large-scale digital printing of textiles was beginning to make borrowings from and re-workings of historical imagery feasible and Connor saw how he could use that complex graphic imagery within the new interior. Perhaps the idea may have been prompted by the memory of his and Westwood's first encounter, when he had pasted collages of the photocopied ruins of bombed out Dresden on to the walls of Seditionaries. Westwood's professional progression was reflected not only in her change of address but in the content of the images he now used; bombed ruins were superseded by the gilded interiors of Baroque palaces.

For the Adam Ant flat he had had bespoke fabrics with hand-printed Classical imagery. Now digital printing allowed him to use more intricate imagery – computers found intricacies no more difficult to reproduce than simplicities. Walls were draped with lengths of fabric that, like those in the Ant flat, spilled across the floor, which was 'tiled' in 60-cm-square MDF panels, also digitally printed with matching imagery and given a transparent protective seal. The shop was on two floors. The Baroque patterns were used at street level and the images of hanks of blonde hair on the lower.

The strategy offered the possibility of printing new wall fabrics and floor tiles to align with new collections of clothes. Whatever the collection, the trompe-l'oeil effect of layered pattern had some of the grandeur of the hall of mirrors at Versailles and some of the entertaining confusion of a hall of mirrors in a funfair.

Chain gang (2)

Although Connor's kind of risk-addicted client was becoming hard to find in the 1990s, he had not lost his knack for attracting those who operated on the edges of prevailing business practice. One such was Peter Simon who had, after time spent on the hippie trail and selling ethnic clothing from a stall in Portobello street market, opened his first Monsoon shop in 1974. Monsoon grew to become a chain that graduated from 'boho-chic' to more mainstream lines with 450 shops in the UK and 800 across the world. In the 1990s it was facing competition from phalanxes of main street brands that were investing in impressive

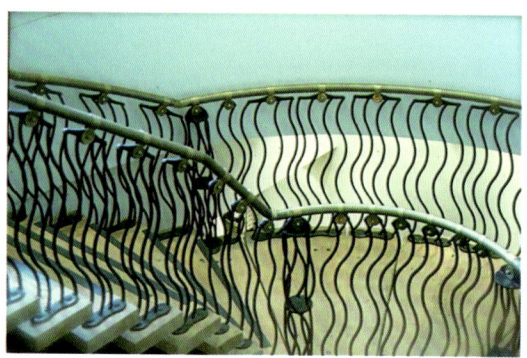

The Monsoon chain: a palette of materials and well-wrought detail that matched anything on the high street and in couture boutiques.

interiors in strategically located flagship stores. Simon knew Connor's work from the 1980s and saw him as the designer who could give his chain a distinct identity.

Over the decade Connor designed Monsoon interiors in eight high-profile locations: four in London, one in Norwich (perhaps the most boho of British cities) and one each in Boston, Copenhagen and Dublin. The interiors were spectacular amalgams of spatial drama and well-crafted detail, to complement, he said, the quality 'inherent in the Monsoon merchandise'.[40] The quality of interior rivalled that of more expensive couture boutiques and they traded well. His connection to the brand went beyond the serial designing of its interiors. He also designed the company's offices and attended strategic meetings to offer opinions on how the physical elements of the chain should consolidate its image. The work was not lucrative but it provided a steady income and helped finance the greater input needed for the one-off projects that did come along.

After Monsoon, one might have expected Connor to attract other fashion chains but as a one-man practice that specialised in unpredictable solutions he was out of sync with the times. Stubbornly individualistic shopkeepers with small radical boutiques were disappearing. The big chains functioned with layers of interlocking management and had their own commissioning strategists who gravitated to design companies that had equally complex teams of fashion retail specialists and tranches of young staff. Few of them knew about Connor's work ten years earlier. They had a formula that worked and collectively fashion retailers and retail designers concocted strong and successful interiors that relied on consensus rather than the hunch of an individual. David Connor Design did not look like a 1990s retail design company. For all his success with Monsoon, he would appear to be just a little too old and he was not in a position to surround himself with fashion-conscious young assistants who could make a bridge for him to the fashion brands. And he did not particularly wish to do that. He wanted clients who were opinionated individuals with whom he could interact.

Live!

Given that his early projects were tonally and predominantly grey one might, in the light of his next major project, suppose that the Atlantic had whetted his appetite for colour. He had won a limited competition, to design the headquarters for Live TV, a new cable television company based in a neverland on the 24th floor of a tower in Canary Wharf, the commercial development that was colonising a huge area of London's redundant docklands. Live TV was an initiative by the Mirror Newspaper Group, which was housed on the floors below, to provide a cable television channel that would operate as a subsidiary to the newspaper and would concentrate on sport in general and football in particular. It was headed by Kelvin MacKenzie, the boisterous but hugely successful editor of tabloid newspapers, and Janet Street-Porter, who had studied architecture for a few years in the 1960s before transitioning smoothly into print journalism and then television, where she had created radical youth-orientated programmes for the BBC and ITV. Apart from MacKenzie and Street-Porter, the staff was inexperienced and ill-equipped to refine an appropriate formula for a medium without precedence in the UK.

Street-Porter made a point of extravagantly caricaturing her working class accent and, following her time in architecture school, was a loud advocate of radical modern design. She was just the sort of champion who could make sure that Connor's proposal would not be dismissed by management from the floor below. He found her 'lovely to work with', unlike the Mirror Group pragmatists.[41]

Connor's interior was about bustle, informality and operating metaphorically both outside and inside the impermeable studio box. He proposed that the whole floor area should be designed as a potential set with strong bright colours that both defined and broke up flat walls and would become the station's on-screen identity. Walls were washed by lights of matching hues to intensify colours, some were curved and others slid across the floor to reconfigure performance spaces. Since all areas were potentially sets, everything in the office had to be ready to feature on screen. All computer monitors, which were at the time both bulky and beige, had to be sprayed in appropriate hues. Spraying such delicate machines had to be carried out in controlled conditions by specialists and costs crept higher. The Mirror group would happily have absorbed the cost – had the station's output attracted an audience.

Acoustic priorities prompted padded surfaces and suspended ceilings were abandoned to expose the dense battery of lighting equipment necessary to make programmes. Enormous ventilation ducts were necessary to extract the heat generated by lighting performance areas. Machinery noise had to be reduced. Floor-to-ceiling windows gave panoramic views of London and beyond but added to the problems of environmental control – special blinds were needed to control natural light. Hugely complicated wiring was necessary; an electrical contractor remarked to Connor on the irony of the number of incoming electrical cables that were needed to feed the single distribution cable that took programmes out to the disappointingly small numbers of subscribers.

Connor handled the technological complications of the build with a practical

Live! TV, London: a hybrid of television studio and production offices slotted into the 24th floor of a commercial tower.

Live! TV, London: an eclectic combination of strong colours and incongruous props.

efficiency far greater than anything required for his earlier projects. The task was complicated by his having to comply with Canary Wharf's own standards of construction. Mirror Group were obliged to employ the Canary Wharf construction arm to carry out the building work and, while the imposed specification and designated contractor inflated costs, the obligations had the advantage of taking some of the contract administration away from Connor.

Live TV was ahead of its time – a little too far ahead of its time. There was no established market for cable television in the UK comparable to that in the United States. Before Live! chose to ignore the distinction between what happened in front of and behind the cameras, the mechanisms of production, whether animate or inanimate, were strictly separated and unplanned glimpses of equipment and non-performers were considered embarrassing. Connor's casual approach to what constituted a television set prefigured the much more relaxed attitude that was to prevail in the next century but it was a little too early to take advantage of the digital communication that was to service the whole of the British Isles within ten years as phones with the capacity to record and transmit sound and vision became commonplace tools and high production values suggested a lack of authenticity. Live! had no competitors to help increase a general customer base and provide a context in which it might find an appropriate place. The sporting content was arguably the most serious of the station's output. Street-Porter had been responsible for the non-sporting content and her modest plan included interviews with celebrities, reviews, lifestyle features and reports from events happening across the UK. She had begun with more serious, less tabloid, intentions for programme content but it quickly became apparent that the initial output, which was by no means inclined towards the cerebral, was not attracting customers, and content went crudely and increasingly downmarket. The failure to attract an audience became obvious quickly and Street-Porter left the station four months after its opening in 1994.

Entertainment standards went further downmarket. The most notorious example of this was a 'topless darts' tournament for glamour models and Connor was intrigued on one visit to find a race in progress – for hamsters pulling tiny chariots. In some desperation the company tried to make the most of the office as set and conjured up a soap opera, which also failed. It was called *Canary Wharf*, which may have been symptomatic of the prevailing lack of imagination.

The panache of Connor's design may have been misplaced. Even if the audience had been willing to accept the blurring of performance and backup areas, they would have had trouble with his strong bright colours and abstract patterns. TV-am, a daytime news-orientated broadcaster with lofty intentions, had been launched three years before Live! in a flurry of chic modernity and had been forced to resort to pastel-painted sets of faux domesticity.

It is perhaps not too far-fetched to conclude that not only was Connor's work wasted on the station's average viewers but that the venture might have been more successful had the sets been tackier and a great deal more vulgar. The station closed in 1999.

There was an important after-effect from Live! for Connor, however. His small office socialised with another small office across a shared courtyard and, amongst the other's staff, Kate Darby was spending her formal year out from the Bartlett School of Architecture. She had begun her architectural studies at the comparatively late age of 26, having already taken a degree in Economics at Bristol University and then worked and trained in a photographer's studio. Connor asked her to photograph Live! and the work took two weekends. Thereafter they continued a more romantic liaison. She completed her studies after two more years at the Architectural Association and they married in 1998.

On top

By the end of the decade Connor was feeling 'ground down' by clients and increasingly irritated by their tendency to inveigle him into doing extra work for no extra pay.[42] He was also obliged to arbitrate on their behalf when they wanted to squeeze unpaid work out of builders with whom he tended to sympathise.

In addition to his ongoing work with Monsoon, he took on another consultancy role, with PKS, an architectural practice that worked primarily for commercial developers and had recognised the importance of having specialist input in the face of what it described as 'extensive and dramatic changes in both the architectural and the development worlds'.[43] He enjoyed his role, which was clearly defined, and he was able, and expected, to make and influence decisions. Connor is not by inclination a team player; his ideas are too shaped by idiosyncratic visions and working methods. He had worked well with Powell-Tuck but they were equal partners and, after initial collaboration, they each took control of final resolutions and he had been the ultimate arbitrator on his own work since leaving John Stefanidis 20 years earlier.

He was still dealing with difficult clients on his own projects but it was therapeutic for his PKS work to leave client contact and the mundane obligations of practice to others. After ten years as a one-man practice, calling in ad hoc support as he needed it, it was pleasant to have his responsibilities diluted.

The most spectacular of his projects with PKS was for an addition to the roof of a development of flats above ground-floor shops and restaurants in the chic Primrose Hill area of London.

There are architectural practices that baulk at employing interior design specialists but, particularly amongst those working for residential property developers, there is a recognition, or an obligation imposed by clients anxious to sell their properties, that another, different eye and sensibility is the way to improve the interiors. The doctrinaire Modernist who believes in hard-edged, white empty spaces, who believes that an exterior and interior should be one, will not willingly hand over responsibility to an interior designer but commercial architects are less precious and PKS involved him early in the design process. Villa Zapu did provide him with some architectural credentials but it had, by his standards then, been uncharacteristically white, indoors and out, which may demonstrate that when an architect, or a designer, had grappled with an exterior there is not enough energy left to reboot and think afresh about the interior.

On Primrose Hill he was involved from the beginning in the evolution of the extremely mannered structure that was perched on top of the distinctly more sober lower floors of stock brick that were, for planners, the acceptable face of a building in the area. The cuckoo structure grew from a rational response to the planning requirement that restricted the height of the building as seen from the street. It is an article of faith with developers that they should squeeze maximum accommodation out of every site and the solution to adding another floor was to set the new structure far enough back from the approved parapet to be invisible from the street. The same strategy prompted the gentle slope of the zinc-clad roof, which allowed the ceiling height of the additional floor to rise towards the back of the site, remaining out of sight until it joined the vertical rear wall with a sweeping radius that was also expressed in the interior.

The penthouse was on two floors, the lower behind the approved brick facade and the upper hidden behind the parapet. A stair connecting the entrance on the lower floor to the upper wound around the perimeter of the double height space that separated the sitting and dining areas on the upper level. The spectacle of the enormous room with its unbroken views across the city and the sweep of the roof soffit required nothing more than a relatively restrained selection of furniture.

There had been discussion about how the 120 sq m of the upper floor area should be subdivided but Connor remembers someone asking 'But when do you ever get a 27-m-long room in London?'[44] That question was rhetorical and the enormous space went undivided. The window that ran the 27-m-length of the west elevation looked on to a wide decked terrace with a low hedge that masked the back of the brick parapet that obscured signs of habitation from street level. A wooden floor matched the decking on the terrace and extended the perceived size of the room to even more spectacular dimensions. The terrace and glazing wrapped around the south elevation and sat above a similar glazed wall and broad balcony to the principal bedroom on the floor below. There were three bedrooms and four bathrooms, a gym and a cloakroom on the lower floor, which sits meekly behind the approved brick elevation.

Connor was mildly irritated by the developers' insistence that limestone should be used in all the bathrooms. He concedes that it is a matter of very little importance, but the fact that he remembers the restriction 20 years on confirms that he was not quite cut out to be a developer's designer. It was perhaps not the limestone he objected to but that the decision was not his.

Ex-pats

In 1998, Connor and Darby, who had now completed her part 2 architectural qualification, decided to move to France and live on 140 hectares of land, La Ferme Roland, near Fréjus on the Côte d'Azur, that Darby had inherited. Connor wanted to get away from the pressures of finding and satisfying tiresome clients and they both thought they might try a little property speculation and thus be able to design without client interference. There were a number of potentially lucrative sites on the land and Connor decided that he had garnered just enough experience of developing in the last years of P-TCO to have a go.

They were spared the initial burden of buying a site but other problems quickly became apparent. The land was very beautiful but rigorously protected by planning legislation, and getting permission for any development was difficult. The more important decisions about what they could do on this fragile site would need to be made in Paris and the process took a long time. Darby spoke French but had not the esoteric French necessary to conduct business and deal with unfamiliar building legislation. They continue to work in France and collaborate with local architects as required and with that guidance and insight they have learnt something about the machinations in the local *mairie*. There were also other complications given that part of their land was a protected habitat for tortoises. Other planning retrictions were more familiar: old buildings were to be preserved as a matter of course and new buildings had to ape the old as far as possible.

Le Parc Lord Rendel, Fréjus: the archer in the foreground of the drawing is a centaur and it may have been his strong arm that caused an arrow to overshoot its target and kill the spectator who lies beneath the orange trees.

To win some goodwill with the local authorities they offered to donate a large area of their land to the local authority in Fréjus to make a public park in return for permission to develop other areas they owned within its jurisdiction and they added drawings suggesting how it could be developed. Connor remembered the intoxicating smell of oranges from his visits to Seville and he proposed an orange grove to surround a central plateau designated for sporting recreations, including archery. Connor drew a bird's eye view of the proposal and was unable to resist adding an archer lying dead beneath the trees, an arrow through his heart. It was perhaps not the sort of drawing to sell a project to local authority functionaries. They suggested that the project be named Le Parc Lord Rendel after Darby's great-great-grandfather, who had owned the land. The municipality refused the offer saying that they already had enough parks to maintain and no wish for another. Perhaps it would have been more diplomatic to name the proposal after Fréjus's most distinguished son, the Abbé Sieyès, who had argued for the primacy of the common people rather than after an English milord. The mairie suggested that, if they wished to proceed with their philanthropic gesture, the offer could be made to the higher authority in Paris but, without local support, a proposal to dabble with the local habitat was unlikely to win Parisian approval and a planning quid pro quo would be improbable.

Connor, with his enthusiasm for landscaping, had been excited by the possibilities of the parc. Free of the need to rely on clients, he was keen to indulge his interests. For a boy from a semi-detached house in Birmingham, he persistently found himself in interesting predicaments.

Connor and Darby lived in a former farmhouse that belonged to her mother and Darby upgraded another small farmhouse on their own land, which they rented out. They then converted a not very old structure for storing wine into a dwelling. It was not a distinguished building but sat amongst hummocky hills and venerable trees. Darby thought they should wait until they had evolved a strategy for the whole site but Connor felt it more important to get planning permission for its conversion to a dwelling and to sell it. Darby conceded to his greater experience and he took responsibility for designing it. By excavating a metre below the existing ground floor level, he added a new lower floor that contained five bedrooms. Living and dining spaces were on the upper floor and the entrance area was at an intermediate level between the two new floors. The proposal was given planning permission and, with that, they sold the site.

He and Darby kept themselves busy in France but, after a year and a half, decided to return to the UK. As he had in California, Connor had been quickly disenchanted by the predictability of the climate and had begun to miss London. Living in the countryside was too uneventful. The views remained unwaveringly beautiful but unchanging and people were rarely sighted. It may be that with his early propensity for gloomy gothic interiors he needs less affable weather. When he drew the Seville tower, which in reality looked like baked terracotta clay, it was dark and bleak against an agitated wet, grey sky. And in his second and favourite drawing of the tower it became no more than a detail in a wet, dark landscape. Darby, who had been offered part-time teaching at the Bartlett School of Architecture, was also inclined to favour a return to London

They continue to work in France. Having received planning permission for a residential development on another parcel of their land, they sold the plot and permission to a local developer with a covenant that the houses should be 'Modern' rather than ersatz vernacular. The dwellings sold briskly and appeared to prove that, however chary planning authorities were of anything modernistic, buyers preferred the comforts of the newly built complete with interiors that better accommodated contemporary ways of living and generous windows that framed views. While pleased with the general appearance of the buildings, they were disappointed with the developer's interpretations of detailing. Recognising that little things mean a lot, they have extended the conditions of the covenants on future transferences to developers to include significant details that must be implemented. Such conditions reduce the price they may ask but they are idealists.

La Ferme Roland, Fréjus, France: housing for the elderly, sold with planning permission and a covenant that obliged the developer to respect the details prescribed in the drawings.

not the end

When they returned from France, Connor and Darby, with the addition of their daughter Fleur who had been born in France, moved back into their flat on the top floor of a Victorian terraced house in Notting Hill but, when Grace was born shortly after their return, it began to look ominously small and they began to look for somewhere bigger. They found a house that was a little further from the acceptable quarters of the city than they might have wished. For Connor it looked a little too much like a suburb, without the elegance of Bourneville, and when he learned that leases of flats in the house next door were for sale they offered to buy the two top floors if the freeholder would agree to structural alterations. The freeholder was keen to sell and agreed. Suburbia was evaded.

The new flat posed a dilemma. While conceding that Connor was by far the more experienced and that she was busy with her teaching jobs and motherhood, Darby wanted to be involved in the design of the flat but Connor, accustomed to working on his own, quickly became engrossed in the design process. Darby felt frustrated and took a part-time job in a friend's architectural practice.

Decisions about the new flat were determined by planning restrictions. Initial intentions for a spectacular roof addition were curbed but, as always, restrictions forced a rethink and a solution that required the sort of ingenuity that moves thinking into new territory. Connor's thwarted first intention had been to build what he describes as a 'glass house' with a pitched roof at the upper level.[45] The planners did allow the remodelling of the upper floor – as long as no part of the outcome was visible from the street or surrounding buildings. Denied the possibility of adding structure he put his energy into the roof, the one external surface available to him. The deep plan of the typical London terraced house, with windows only on the narrow front and back elevations, makes for a dark core and his solution was to insert a rooflight that occupied the greater part of the new flat roof and could be rolled back, with technological theatricality, in hot weather.

Connor/Darby flat, London: the rooflight opens above the living and dining floor on the upper level.

Deprived of exterior elements to work with Connor might have released frustrated energy on the interior with, perhaps, something resembling the daubings of the Pirroni flat, but he was 20 years older and the new millennium was not a time for punkisms – or New Romanticisms. Perhaps he anticipated that his young daughters would scribble on the walls and thought that would be quite enough. Perhaps in 2002 the pristine interiors of the space vehicles that had excited him in the film 2001 had crept back into his imagination. If he was indeed transitioning from interior designer to architect then he would have become enraptured with white surfaces.

Unlike the Ant and Pirroni flats – which were conversions within London terraced houses trapped between their own floors and ceilings and restricted to whatever light could be borrowed from the tight corridor of a London street – the rooflight ensured that the centre of the flat was deluged in light and, to crank up the light levels and the drama a little more, beneath the rooflight, he set three long and narrow glazed slots into the dark red/brown wooden floor to feed natural light to the core of the lower floor. He points out that roof lights allow significantly more light to enter a room than do windows in walls.

The existing top floor had been no more than an attic set behind sloping walls to front and back. He retained the meagre 2.3m ceiling height of the upper floor, squeezed under a flat roof that allowed it to crouch below the sightlines of the upper floors of neighbouring houses. The floor-to-ceiling height on the upper floor is less than that on the floor below but claustrophobia is eliminated by the enormous rooflight that covers by far the greater part of the floor area. Darby is pleased that she was able to persuade Connor to adjust the structure to eliminate downstand beams, which would have further lowered and broken up the ceiling plane and the important impression of a single large room.

The upper floor is devoted to living and eating, the lower to bedrooms with the entrance door a further floor below, off the communal stair. The arrival area is no wider than the stair, just big enough to allow the door to swing open. Guests assuming that the entrance door would open directly on to one of the floors of the flat are deflated to find themselves with another flight to climb. Connor excuses the expediency by talking about the exhilaration of light flooding down the stairwell after the trudge through the gloom of the communal stair.

Arrival at the bedroom level offers an upliftingly wide landing area on which borrowed light from the stairwell is augmented by that from the rooflight which filters through a narrow glass strip set into the floor above. At either end of the landing wide doors swing back through 180 degrees to finish flush with the faces of

Connor/Darby flat, London: artificial light from the entrance hall below and natural light filtering through the glazed slots in the floor above illuminate the landing on the bedroom floor.

Connor/Darby flat, London: seats and cupboards occupy the
slots created between vertical windows and sloping roofs.

Connor/Darby flat, London: the apparently random slashes of glass in the floor on the upper level are determined by the layout of bedrooms below. The little ladder in the far corner leads to the roof terrace.

Connor/Darby flat, London: the view from the roof terrace.

cross-walls and reveal the windows in the front and back elevations.

The plan of the bedroom level remains largely unaltered from that of the original building. The main bedroom, to the front, stretches across the width of the house and has its own bathroom set behind the remnant of the existing cross-wall. A second bathroom serves guests and the children, who are accommodated in two additional bedrooms, each with a window to the rear. Glass strips in the ceilings of the bathrooms borrow daylight from the floor above and a frosted glass wall between the shared bathroom and the landing further breaks up the solid wall opposite the stair, and allows a little extra light, filtering in by the ceiling slot, to make a further modest contribution of natural light to the landing. At upper floor level a broad low balustrade protects the stairwell and allows daylight from the skylight to wash its walls.

The upper floor is devoted to living and eating. The exterior wall to the front is a slate-hung mansard roof that slopes back from the original parapet and is punctuated by two vertical dormer windows. Its inner face is squared off, to nullify the mansard's internal slope, by the vertical faces of floor-to-ceiling storage spaces that are hidden behind a floor-to-ceiling stack of white laminate-covered panels. Two built-in seats fill the recesses in front of the existing sliding sash windows. Joints between the various sized panels relieve the expanses of flat whiteness.

When the electrically powered rooflight slides open, the living space becomes an outdoor space. For the times the family needs to have a long view over the surrounding rooftops, Connor squeezed in a small roof terrace, accessed by a steep little metal ladder off the kitchen zone to the rear, an inelegant expediency but one that is not without local precedents. Darby lobbied for a stair but was unable to find a way to incorporate it without sacrificing too much floor area.

They left the flat in 2008 and moved to Herefordshire, 150 miles from London. Darby misses it but felt that children should grow up with 'mud between their toes'. Connor, whom she describes as a 'city boy', continues to adjust.[46]

Hot runs cold

In 2006, another former collaborator re-emerged. Anish Kapoor and Connor had remained close friends but with a new project the dynamic between them changed: they were no longer collaborators, they were commissioner and commissionee. Connor's public profile had declined since Seville, and Kapoor had become an important, and wealthy, international artist. He was spending more time in exotic locations and decided that he wanted to build a new house in the Bahamas. He asked Connor to design it.

The best island houses had tended to be in an English Colonial style. They had charm but both Kapoor and Connor wanted something new, not necessarily Modern but certainly something attuned to the demands of contemporary lotus-eating.

Connor worked on proposals for three different buildings on three different sites over a four-year period. One project got as far as the pouring of foundations before Kapoor lost interest and sold the site. He could afford to be capricious, and during the necessarily protracted design process he would become restless and want to move on. He would stumble on another site, be excited by it and, without the useful inhibitor of a clear budget, buy it. His own work was three-dimensional and large and it would have been strange had he not had some preconceptions, however vaguely defined, of what the house should be, and delay while Connor searched to find what lurked at the back of his mind allowed Kapoor to change his.

Meeting the practical requirements was not difficult but a solution that worked for client and context was hard to find. Thomas Lundstrom had thought the evolution of Zapu was slow but in the end had realised that the time Connor spent sifting amongst possibilities was necessary to achieve his extraordinary dwelling. Connor had learnt from making Zapu but he was not inclined to recycle ideas. During the developmental period he spent on Kapoor's various houses he had also begun to drift away from the task of providing a bespoke solution and had become interested in the particularities of designing on, and for, the island. He was becoming engrossed in his own agenda and not getting any closer to what Kapoor thought he wanted.

Building on the island is expensive. The Bahamas attracts the rich because it levies no income taxes but it does substitute high import taxes and most building materials are imported. Those avoiding one tax are reluctant to pay another and, consequently, even amongst the wealthy, there is a tendency to make do and mend. The golf buggies that are useful for the short commutes on the island are patched up when they break down.

The native Bahamians, the poor and the not quite so poor, generally live in timber shacks vulnerable to hurricanes, but the flimsy structures are easily rebuilt. The better-off natives and incomers favour brick and concrete, which offer bulwarks against the milder hurricanes. Older one and two storey dwellings usually have verandas that offer cool places to sit and keep sunlight from penetrating interiors. After Zapu and his time spent in the South of France, Connor knew something about living in relentless sunlight. In the Bahamas, he also learnt the importance of shelter from the winds that blew in from the sea and create esoteric

Kapoor house, Bahamas: a sketch that confirms the influence of local vernacular housing.

priorities for those building on the island. Hurricanes and high winds are the great threat to modestly constructed houses, ripping off roofs and tearing them from their foundations, so new houses are built on deep concrete piles with bulbous bases that lock them into the earth. Window glass needs to be strong enough to resist the impact of outdoor furniture hurled against it by winds that can rush into buildings through broken windows and blow roofs off from below.

Modest island dwellings tend to be clad in brightly painted timber boarding. It is this last type, and the rudimentary shacks, that Connor most obviously refers to in his series of proposals. He concluded that timber was an appropriate building material. It could be harvested on the island and would lend itself to evolving a style appropriate to the island.

On the last site Connor worked on Kapoor wanted a house for himself and guest houses that might be rented. The drawings for these modest dwellings are typical of those Connor made throughout the four-year cycle: monochromatic with repetitive pencil lines that represent timber cladding and corrugated tin roofs. They are less about his signature sketches that suggest allusions and moods and more like those of an architect, with clear delineations of the practical considerations that shape ideas and a little more respect for the laws of perspective. In them each little building sits

Kapoor House, Bahamas: speculation about assembling a sizeable single house from a collection of small visually discrete elements.

beneath its own steeply pitched roof, flanked by shallower lean-to mono-pitches. The units are grouped around courtyards that provide shade and shadows. The collection suggests a hamlet in a clearing and he allowed himself a tower, which was also timber clad, with a steeply pitched roof.

Perhaps the pace of the design process was too slow for Kapoor or perhaps as the various versions developed he began to form his own, different idea of what he wanted the house to be. Perhaps he felt that Connor was becoming lost in his own version of a Bahamian vernacular that referred to the simplest housing stock and would determine a way of living that he did not relish. He wanted a house not an architectural manifesto. So he ended Connor's involvement and appointed another architect, from within their mutual circle, who gave him concrete and glass.

Connor was upset to be dismissed. Leaving aside matters of friendship, he had been increasingly excited by each iteration of the building. He was desperate to see it built but had been prepared to go on re-thinking it as long as there was the expectation of its being built. He would have applied himself equally diligently had Kapoor succumbed to buying another site. He had come to see the project not as a one-off holiday retreat, but as a prototype for appropriate, and sustainable, Bahamian housing and welcomed the opportunity to

Kapoor house, Bahamas (digital rendering): the simplicity of vernacular construction is implied by the diagrammatic expression of structure.

Kapoor house, Bahamas (digital rendering): clear separation of elements breaks down the house's bulk.

refine that. He wanted badly to test a prototype. He also entertained the hope that the finished house would bring other Caribbean projects and wondered if he might relocate to the islands to deal with a deluge of commissions. One might suspect that he would become bored with another predictably perfect climate, give or take a few hurricanes.

The proposals had become, almost, real for him and his sketching and two-dimensional drawings were becoming sublimations. He wanted to see the finished article and when he realised that the vision would not be built he had photorealistic digital images made of what would have been the last and most refined of the proposals. The images reveal that the simple structures that had been suggested in the early pencil sketches mislead. The evolved forms are much more sophisticated than re-interpretation of generic shacks implies. The house sits on a rise overlooking the sea, and walls of windows and the terraces beyond them allow for basking in ocean views. The tower has mutated into a room that seems to float on the thick surrounding vegetation. The courtyards sit lower, shaded by overhanging roofs and vegetation.

The structure is wonderfully delicate, ostensibly as ephemeral as the fragile huts of the poor. The principles and details of the timber construction are clearly displayed and components are painted white and make the most of sun and shade to create a simple, rational decorative language. The evolved design is about the separation of elements and that does suggest the delicacy and fragility of vernacular huts. Over-sailing roofs screen rooms from sunlight and appear to sit lightly on the glass walls beneath them. This lightness is most emphatically expressed in the manner in which the very visible floor joists of the 'tower' room sit on top of white painted steel beams, which are in turn supported on round white-painted steel columns. The system is reiterated in the exposed timber joists of the roof and the delicacy of the exposed structural timbers makes the thick green vegetation that covers the hill on which the house sits seem heavy and solid. Delicacy is further emphasised by the thin wooden slats that filter sun from the interior. The exterior is white and the interior is white; tonal variations are left to the sun. The interior melds into the internalised courtyards.

Connor had become frustrated with most of his clients before retreating to France but he was perhaps most disenchanted by the abrupt end of the Kapoor house. He felt let down by being substituted and saw the time spent evolving and resolving the principles that had so excited him as a waste of four years. It is a frustration unique to ambitious architects: they inhabit the buildings they design intimately, in their imaginations, and when ideas are not translated into realities the disappointment

Kapoor House, Bahamas (digital rendering): rooms with enormous sea views are built around courtyards that provide retreats from the sun – and wind.

of not seeing the vision manifested can be wearingly intense. The divergence between his perception and Kapoor's is clearly seen in his successor's proposal that was built. It is described as a studio house, the long, low slot of windows that look out to sea is set deep in projecting concrete planes. An equally solid but separate little cube appears to be perched on the vegetation and also looks out to sea. One might suggest these solids and the voids are the kind of architectural gesture that gets described as 'sculptural'. Connor's proposal had more to do with vernacular architecture, shaped by the logic of its context and construction. It was a building shaped by tradition; it had all the poetry of his best work but the voice was restrained. He says that when clients and designer share a vision they are a good team. For this project he and Kapoor did not share a vision.

Very post-punk

In 2017 Westwood decided to revamp the Mayfair shop. She now had four small shops in London and had just opened two bigger 'flagship' stores in New York and Paris. These were quite unlike the Mayfair 'boutique'; their large areas of floor were punctuated by rows of hanging rails. They were elegant but cautious by Westwood's standards, lacking in intimacy and bland, in the manner of flagship stores everywhere. They seemed to be more about good retailing practice than expressing the provocative personal style and opinions of their founder. She was the eponymous head of a global brand in which many had financial stakes and decisions were necessarily being influenced by those whose role it was to maximise turnover. Westwood had become a doyenne and now had customers who were not the subversive youths that had lounged about in Seditionaries but she had resisted changing the World's End shop for 30 years – it remained a memorial to her break from punk and her first step towards haute couture. She began as a punk and has remained punkish, promoting provocative political positions. She seemed to want another edgy shop to call her own and sent again for Connor who knew how to complement idiosyncrasy.

He stuck to his conviction that the interesting things about the World's End shop had been those elements retained from his first drawings: the clock racing backwards and the sloping floor, the surreal and the disconcerting. He liked the way the slope had affected the way customers were obliged to use their bodies which was, he thought, a parallel to how clothes require their wearers to adjust their bodies.

He had visited the Venice Biennale the year before and been excited by an acoustically dead room. His ideas were, however, as much about sound as silence but he began with the exterior and proposed a canopy over the length

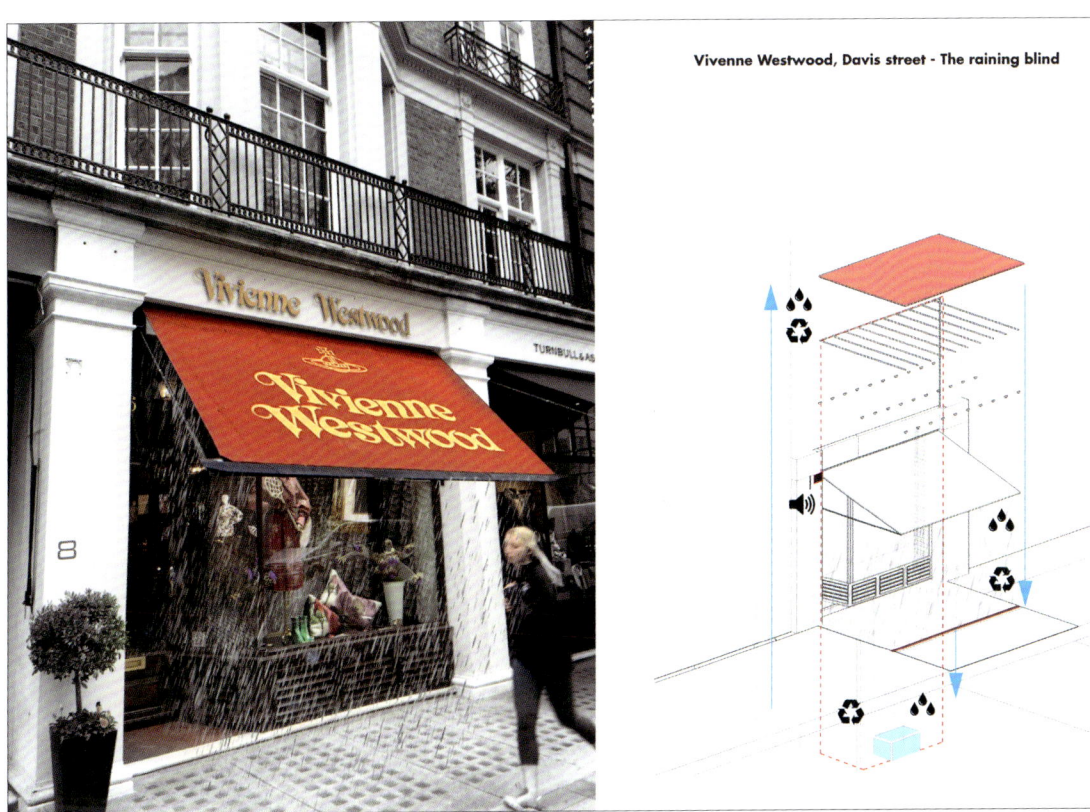

Vivienne Westwood revisited, Davies Street, London:
the canopy 'rains' on the street, on the hour.

Vivienne Westwood revisited, Davies Street, London: a section showing the acoustically 'dead' ground floor and the acoustically 'live' basement.

of the shop front. Canopies are designed to keep rain off; his was designed to deliver rain. He proposed that on every hour a loud speaker would announce 'looks like rain' and on that cue drops of water would fall from the underside of the canopy. It was his first work for Westwood since World's End and the huge clock may have been at the back of his mind but the allusion he cited was to the mechanical figures that emerge from clock faces on venerable public buildings to strike bells and mark hours, attracting small crowds who gather to enjoy the brief spectacle. He wanted to create a modest tourist attraction. It was fanciful but he did not ignore practicalities. The shop owned a metre-wide stretch of pavement along its frontage and in the basement below he planned to collect and recycle his 'raindrops'.

When he moved inside he was as concerned as ever to create 'mood'. On the ground floor level he intended to make an anechoic space, one where absorbent surfaces on walls, floor and ceiling would eliminate the reflection of sound waves to create an (almost) acoustically dead space. The nature of activities within a shop make total deadening impossible but he did enough to affect customers' aural equilibrium. Absorbent materials and devices offered an eccentric palette of finishes. Clothes would have helped absorption.

Downstairs he went to the other extreme and aimed for a 'live' acoustic that needed hard, flat, resonant surfaces. He settled for thin metal skins with a resonating void behind them. He wanted to use the bright steel sheet from which baked bean tins are fashioned. The materials palette threatened to have something punk about it. Clothes would not have helped resonance.

Westwood was enthusiastic but somewhere in the hierarchy of her eponymous company a halt was called. Connor claims to have been relieved that the project was aborted. He had set himself some serious practical problems and he was unsure how to solve them, but in that it was no different from every one of his other projects and he had always found the ways and means to get outrageous things done.

The shop promised to be as bizarre as Seditionaries, perhaps more outré because of its location and because it was not aimed at a clientele of disaffected youths. That Westwood would approve it is a tribute to her perennial instinct to be disruptive and that Connor could propose such a thing suggests that his instinct for finding the extraordinary is undimmed. Neither he nor Westwood appear to have a capacity to grow old gracefully. In the pious and pompous world of couture, and the interiors in which it is sold, a cautious consensus prevails and Connor and Westwood seem unable to subscribe to it.

Folly

A consensus of dictionary definitions declares that a folly is ornamental, frequently a tower or a mock-Gothic ruin, built in a ducal garden or parkland. It should have no practical function and therefore from a philistine, or Modernist, perspective it is a waste of money. It could be argued that recent buildings that have relied for their identity on a contorted profile, whether they are art galleries or office blocks, have something of the folly about them but a folly is required to be something more than attention-seeking. Lavish spending is not enough. It needs to have something romantic about it. The guest tower at Villa Zapu and the Building for a Void meet most of the dictionary criteria. One could make arguments that the flat for Adam Ant, which was romantic and implied incipient ruin, and that for Marco Pirroni, which had something of graffitied abandonment about it, were also follies, self-indulgences by aristocrats of pop. Perhaps accommodating a pair of monks on the roof of one's house is a folly. Perhaps an enormous rooflight that retracts at the press of a button is another.

Evidence might suggest that when a project lends itself to folly then Connor's drawing becomes more intense, as he tries to make tangible the world of his imagination. He had no need to make the drawings he did of the Building for a Void, no need to transport it graphically from Seville to its imaginary spit of wet desolate land. Follies, whatever he might call them, seem to occupy his thoughts. It is not difficult to imagine that his enthrallment goes back to the romantic books and pictures he enjoyed as a child.

Connor was obviously the man to go to if one wanted to step outside the Modernistic boxes that were on offer from professionals ready to toe the prevailing stylistic line but, since Seville, no client had invited him to trip the light fantastic. And so he sought out excuses to indulge his taste for follies.

Beside the sea

The Medway Estuary and Marshes is a bleak area on the Kent coast that is the habitat of the singular varieties of wildlife that thrive in salt marshes, and does not attract casual human intrusion. (Charles Dickens, who knew the area, used it as the location for the first terrifying encounter between the boy Pip and the convict Magwitch in *Great Expectations*.) The Medway local authority, in collusion with the RIBA, held a competition to design the Will Adams Ecological Centre, which it was hoped would help convince potential visitors that the area had charms. (Will Adams was a near-forgotten local hero who, in the 1600s, was the first Englishman to sail to

Will Adams Ecological Centre, Medway Marshes, Kent:
the timber-boarded bird-watching tower.

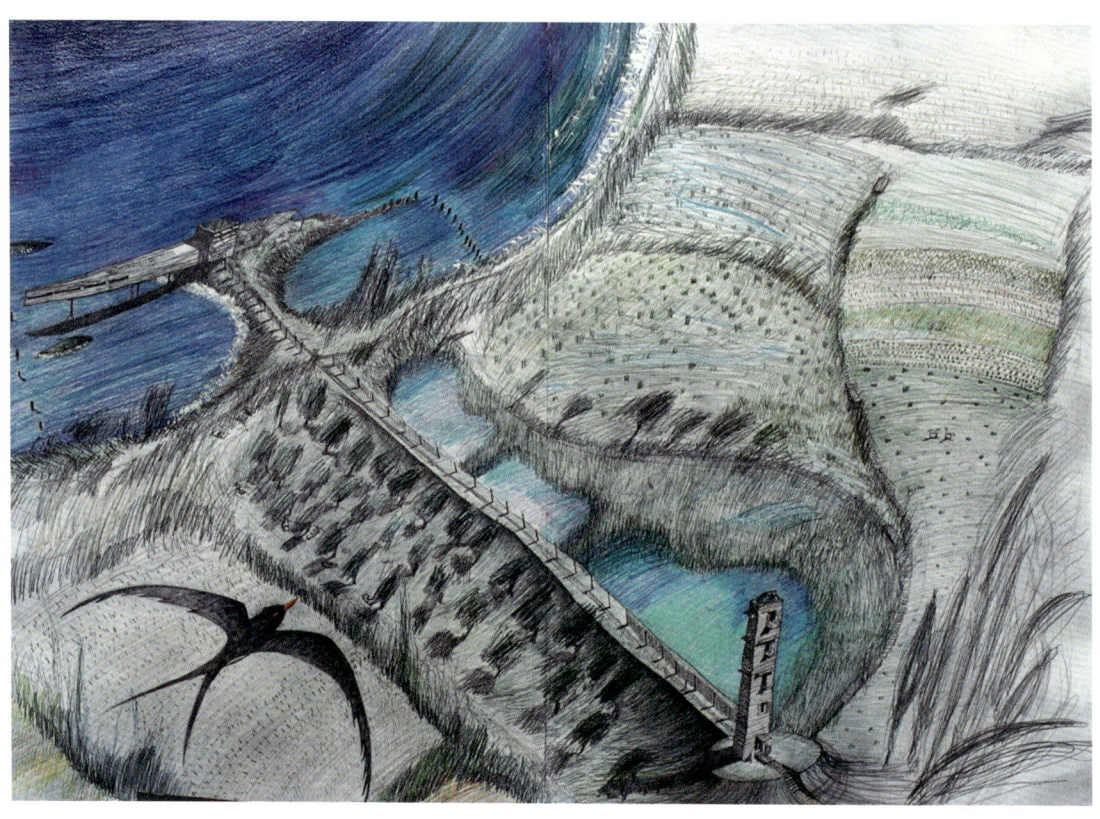

Will Adams Ecological Centre, Medway Marshes, Kent:
a decked walkway links the tower to the long low observation jetty.

Japan, where he became a samurai and never returned to Medway.)

However tenuous its pretext, it was a project to whet Connor's appetite, a landscaping project bigger than Le Parc Lord Rendel and ripe for a folly. He proposed a tall, thin tower clad in timber, pierced with openings and projecting decks for bird watching, crowned with an observatory to take advantage of the dark marsh skies. The tower sat on a raised mound, a little like that for Zapu's guest house, ornamental and monumental, fragilely defying the winds that whipped across the marshes. It marked one end of a long walkway, raised on an embankment above tidal high water and ending in an enclosed jetty, at right angles to it, that looked rather like a boat hovering above the sea, and a little like a stretched version of Villa Zapu itself. The landscaping showed that he had an appetite for earth-moving that was at least the equal of Capability Brown's. His entry was placed third and he was a little consoled that the winning project was never built.

Deep in the forest

In Herefordshire, the Connor/Darby household sits on the edge of a heavily wooded common close to Croft Castle, a crenellated country house in grounds rumoured to have been designed by Capability Brown. The Hall, its grounds and the Common are owned by the National Trust and in 2015 they invited a number of artists and designers to propose additions that would encourage visitors to walk in Croft Castle's extensive grounds. Connor joined forces with Mark Richards, a sculptor who also lived on the Common, and they chose to construct a folly for a 14-acre lake that lay in the middle of the now thickly wooded grounds. Richards called the proposal *The Decorative Hermit and his Machine for Drawing*.

It was a bizarre collusion by two provocatively creative spirits who happen to be neighbours and who happen to not quite fit the nominal professional slots that they have been allocated. Richards is a public figure sculptor who specialises in precise depictions of his subjects. His sitters have included Johnny Rotten of the Sex Pistols, a curious link to Connor via Malcolm McLaren. When not engaged in what is very traditional artistic practice he is an occasional performance artist. He began to offer himself as a hermit in 2010 when he sat amongst the Common's trees without clothes, food, water or shelter and waited for visitors to supply essentials for his three-day vigil. Five years later he was ready to pursue the idea further.

Connor designed a floating hermitage for Richards in which he would spend nine days drawing and contemplating nature. Richards called it *Hermitcraft*. It was an extraordinary amphibious building which, with its incumbent

The Floating Hermitage, Croft Castle, Herefordshire:
a structure of timber boarding and shingles.

The Floating Hermitage, Croft Castle, Herefordshire: the interior open to the drawing platform, a bottle of wine suggests that communing with Nature should not preclude self-indulgence.

The Floating Hermitage, Croft Castle, Herefordshire: a digital rendering.

hermit, would provide those National Trust visitors who would come across it while tramping through the woodland from nearby Berrington Hall with a spectacle equivalent to those little follies and faux ruins, with or without hermits, that were sprinkled in the parks of country estates for the diversion of their owners and their guests. Capability Brown had laid out a path through the Berrington grounds for horse-drawn carriages so that grandees, who were disinclined to walk, could enjoy the vistas he had created. That path led past the small lake on which Richards would embark.

Connor's little structure might be classified as a modest tower. It was a beehive-shaped two-storey cabin clad in sycamore shingles and built on a raft that also supported a swivelling dentist's chair that could be extended over water or land – a simple structure, made from the wood that grew on the estate. If the 'primitive hut' offered by the Abbé Laugier in the middle of the 18th century was the progenitor of Classical architecture then Connor's primitive hut, if it was not the organic precursor of the blobs that are today's 'iconic' buildings, was their modestly scaled, environmentally friendly equivalent.

Richards' intention was to draw from the dentist's chair and, for the duration of the performance and in the presence of nature, he anticipated being inspired by observation and drawing to contemplate his own humility. The vessel would be his means to that end. He classified it as a 'habitation, observatory and studio that functions like a hide but which itself is being watched' – by the visitors who would make their little pilgrimages to observe it and its curious inmate.[47] There was something of Thoreau's Walden Pond about the exercise and its intent.

A live, albeit sedentary, human exhibit was an escalation of content for the artistic installations that the National Trust customarily offered as visitor attractions, and a raft was a lot for a National Trust committee to accept and it lost to a more familiar 'intervention' in the woods. Connor, drawing on his entrepreneurial instinct, suggested that while Richards' initial performance would draw crowds, the 'building' could be given a more permanent life. It was, he suggested, a curious object that would continue to provide visitors with an incentive to walk in the woods and could have a prolonged existence as a retreat for other artists. He also suggested that it could make money if rented out to anyone wishing to trifle with the life of a hermit for a few days. It was big enough to accommodate two at a squeeze. Visitors would paddle, in a coracle, to the hut which would have a bottled gas-fired cooker and a chemical lavatory, those mainstays of a life of quiet contemplation. The logistics of cleaning it, fuelling it and emptying its chemical lavatory, exacerbated by the possibility of a visitor drowning, may well have sunk the proposals chances but at an exhibition

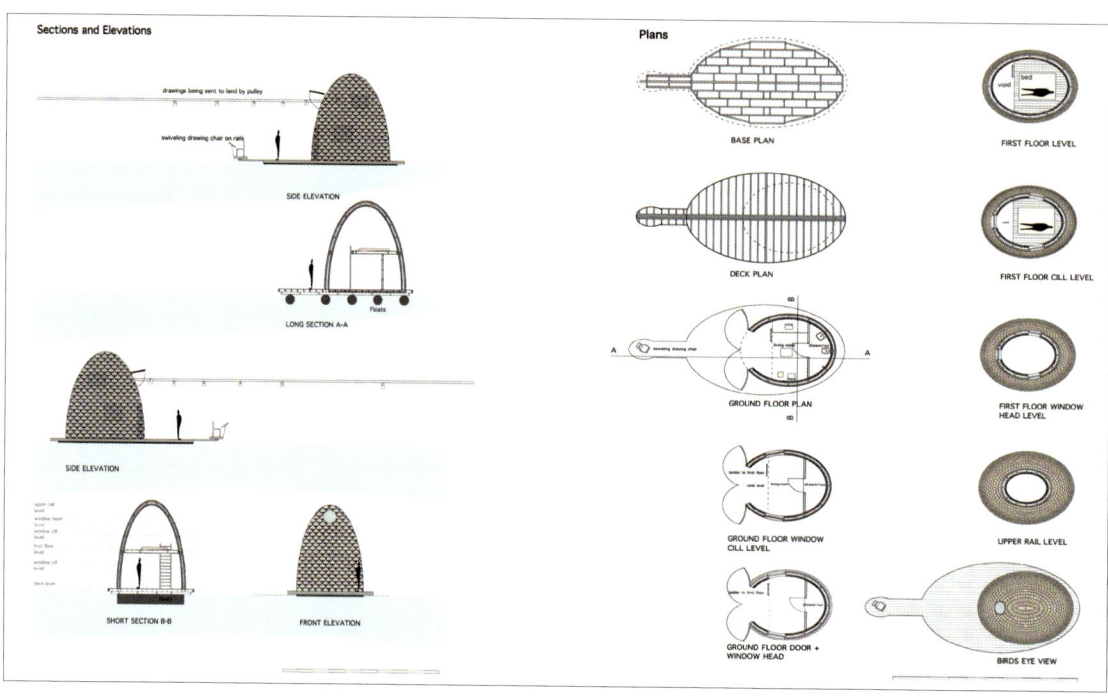
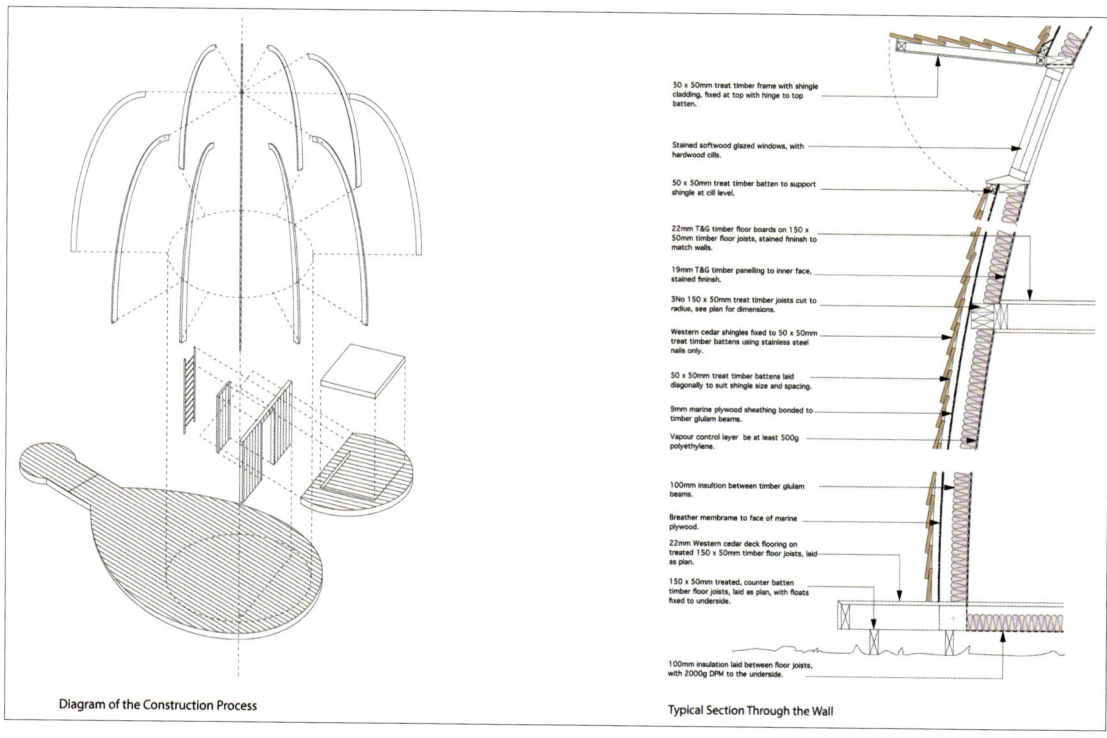

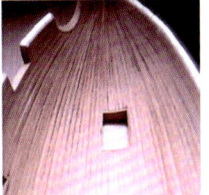

The Floating Hermitage, Croft Castle, Herefordshire: detailed technical drawings (opposite); a half model (top) which perhaps suggests a rustic affinity with Building for a Void; and an aerial perspective (above).

of the commissioned proposals a number of visitors declared their interest in experiencing it. At the very least it was an alternative to glamping. Connor also commissioned Anahi Copponex to design a bright red monk's habit, a prototype for the habit that might be adopted by those seeking the hermitic experience.

A tomb for a monument

In 1910 Adolf Loos announced that 'only a very small part of architecture belongs to the realm of art: the tomb and the monument.'[48] It was another fusillade in his argument against architectural ornament. His proposition was that everything other than the tomb and the monument was just plain ordinary building and could, he conceded, be decorated, to lift plebeian spirits. He was effectively declaring that any building that had a mundane practical purpose could not be considered art. Modernist architects appreciated his stricture against ornament but, given that commissions for tombs and monuments were few, decided that a concrete bus station should be classified as monumental.

In 2012 Connor and Darby began collaborating on a project that could be described as both a monument and a tomb – but not as Loos would have recognised them. Their house in Herefordshire was listed and included in the listing were the fragile remains of an old, chronically dilapidated cottage and the footings of what had probably been a stable. The ruin was picturesque and while it is pleasant to own a ready made folly the building was uncomfortably close to becoming rubble; the roof had collapsed, the walls were crumbling and trees and wild plants sprouted from its remains. It was impossible to say if it had once had aesthetic merit; not enough of it remained.

The sensible solution was to demolish it and perhaps build something new on its site but its being listed complicated that option. If it were to fall down there would be no automatic right to build on its footprint; a restriction to ensure that owners of listed ruins are deterred from disposing of them in a choreographed accident. As a ruin it had little value; as a house with potential for obtaining planning permission it was valuable. The solution was to repair the ruin, but making it structurally sound and weatherproof would have been absurdly, disproportionately expensive and the cost would have made the future possibility of a profit on its sale unlikely. Leaving aside the financial consideration, Connor and Darby were not keen to have a crumbling ruin next to their house but finding a solution to its reclamation did offer them the opportunity they had sought in France, to build on their own terms.

When discussing responsibility for the project today they agree that, after conversations with a conservation officer about their options, their decision to protect the remnants by building a new weather-tight shed around it had emerged organically and simultaneously.

The solution was not unprecedented – it was based on the principle that protects terracotta armies and fragments of Roman walls within new structures – but they took the idea to an extreme conclusion. They proposed to make a tomb (the shed) to encase a monument (the cottage). Darby gives credit to Connor for recognising 'the power of keeping clods of earth' and for advocating preserving everything as they found it, rather than cleaning away the casual accretions of centuries to exhibit what might or might not be the original core of the original building.[49] There was, he argued, nothing to indicate definitively the nature of the building when first built or the lifestyle of its first inhabitants. He argued for the random accumulation that told something of the building's evolution. So they kept the crumbling walls and the rusty nails driven into timber beams; they kept the old birds' nests, the rags of hessian sacking and the odd pieces of decaying string that hung, randomly and redundantly, from walls and beams. They left cobwebs in situ. They were recognising that pedantic restoration would create something false. They would keep the house as it had survived and add its next phase. Reverting only to its supposed beginnings would be to destroy traces of the equally legitimate and interesting moments in between then and now. It meant accepting the desiccated dead bats, the ivy that was alive when the work began and died when it was incarcerated in the 'protective' shell.

They argued that their building could not be authentic if it interfered with what existed and that the necessary new elements should be distinctly of their time. They accepted that the new would not be valued until it aged. Until then the new was the ruin's carer. They were aligning themselves with Peter York who, also in 2012, in *Authenticity Is a Con* proposed that once one stops curating the past 'you can get on with life – and embrace the modern world.'[50] The conservation officer accustomed to forcing reluctant householders to retain redundant period pieces was delighted by the idea and the solution gave the planners little to which they might take exception – other than perhaps a suspicion that their principles were being discreetly mocked. (Planners are often maligned. They can be the grains of sand that aggravate an architectural pearl into being.)

Connor, with the bit between his teeth, argued that the 'tomb' should be a corrugated tin shed. Darby thought he might be pushing their luck but the conservation officer was an admirer of old corrugated huts and Connor discovered that corrugated tin, with its classic wavy profile, had been invented in the 1820s. It was not modern – but it was fashionable.

Croft Lodge Studio, Herefordshire: the remains, as found.

Croft Lodge Studio, Herefordshire: the retained gable will form one wall of the workplace that will occupy the footprint of the old stables.

The planning application proposed accommodation for guests and a studio that would be shared by Darby's architectural and Connor's design practices. all to be contained within a single structure. Corrugated tin helped the argument; it was not without precedent in the countryside and contrasted well with the newer aluminium cladding that blights farmyards. It was elegantly petite compared to the monstrous new agricultural sheds. Half of it protects the old, the other half is the studio, built on the outline of the vanished stable. Occupying the stable's footprint allowed the gable wall to sit on the boundary line with the common.

The entombed ruin provides accommodation for guests in the little rooms of the original building where they may bang their heads on low beams, to be compensated by the pleasure of finding the relics of its past. What it lacks in comforts it repays with romantic decrepitude. The ground floor has a sitting room, a dining area and a kitchen. The upper level is for sleeping.

The studio is a tall, well-lit, precisely built and pristinely white room with a wood-burning stove and a large work table shared with assistants. The gable wall is dominated by a tall east-facing window. Horse riders on the common look in and wave as they pass. The other walls are windowless but windows in the sections protecting the old building are aligned

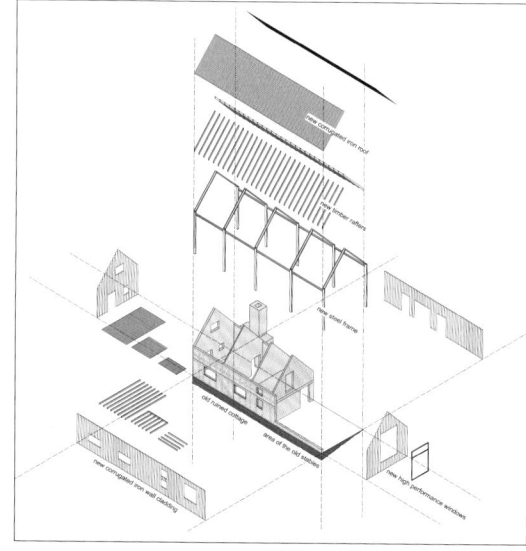

Croft Lodge Studio, Herefordshire: the strategy.

Croft Lodge Studio, Herefordshire: the remains of the original house's gable are the fourth wall of the otherwise precise white workplace.

Croft Lodge Studio, Herefordshire: the new corrugated skin.

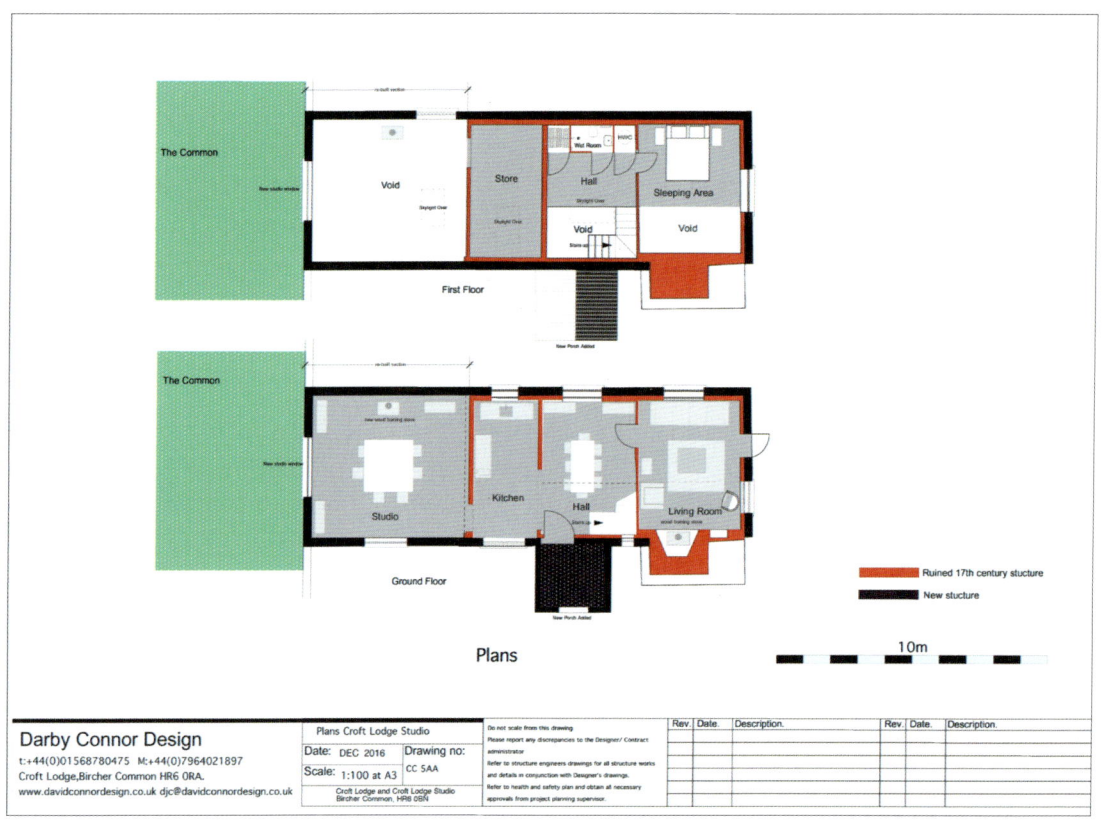

Croft Lodge Studio, Herefordshire: the plans.

with the original cottage windows which, to varying degrees, have retained their glass and timber frames. Some original openings contain the twisted remains of decorative cast-iron frames and suggest that, sometime in its undocumented existence, the little building had some social standing.

If the planning process was streamlined, construction was slow. It took the best part of four years. Connor and Darby each had other projects to deal with and they were their own clients and could take time to make the very esoteric decisions that construction and reclamation threw up. The pace of the work was partially determined by their workforce. They employed only one regular, a Slovenian jack of all trades, who each day walked 40 minutes across the common to get to work and 40 minutes to get home again. It was a ritual that was something like the commute to work of those who had built and adapted the old structure. Connor was primarily responsible for making decisions about how the new could be threaded into the old and he could take time. There were no impatient trades working to a fixed price and no client demanding to be in by Christmas.

The corrugated carapace that was the project's public face may look, at first glance, like a standard metal barn but its dimensions and proportions were determined by the evidence extrapolated from the remains of the cottage. It is tall and the angle of its steeply pitched roof gives it an elegance that distances it from the squat pitches of the modern shed.

Traditional corrugated tin has sometimes been used for buildings of slightly higher status, modest seaside bungalows, village meeting halls and places of worship for esoteric religious sects. Whether Loos would have conceded that such expedient structures belonged in the category of monument is doubtful.

Connor and Darby wanted their cladding to be black, the traditional tin shed finish in the area. Modern corrugated products came with that colour option but the plasticised finish was too glossy for Darby. She insisted that it should be finished with traditional paint with a less reflective finish. Connor was given responsibility for finding someone to carry out the process and, after a wide-ranging search, found a local company that could do it. Many of the specialist trades and suppliers they used were local, partly driven by their concern to reduce carbon footprint but, perhaps more importantly, to have the opportunity to talk through ways to achieve their particular aesthetic ends, and it was useful to visit workshops and to have prototypes made.

Darby took responsibility for detailing the new structure. Agricultural sheds are bought off shelves and their standard detailing for openings, corners and eaves is clever but necessarily generalised and visually crude, designed to be assembled at speed and to repel weather. The scale of components is wrong for a small dwelling. She evolved a number of delicate flashings that were made locally, after considerable discussion and prototyping.

The protective skin, like its farm building equivalents, was fixed to portal frames set out over four bays, two and a half of which were assigned to cover the ruin. It is pragmatic but the simple precision of form seems more like an architectural diagram than an expedient solution.

Their engineer had no trouble designing the portal frame of the shed but no formulae for calculating the structural capabilities of decaying timbers. They resorted to hunches. The existing upper floor was partially intact but, since some joists had failed, the whole was upgraded to a single structural slab by sheets of 18 mm plywood screwed and glued to the best of the surviving joists. There were other elements that looked, and were, vulnerable. Timbers were reinforced with bolts and steel straps which, like all the expediencies in the cottage's previous existences, were left to speak for themselves. They look new but will mellow in their own time.

The process of erecting the shed/skin over the remains of the cottage was complicated. When the structural frame had been erected close to the ruined walls the inner skin could only be fixed from outside, which required ingenuity, dexterity and special screwdrivers. With that in place, insulation could be inserted from the outside and the outer skin attached. The space between external skin and existing wall was a useful distributing zone for electrical cabling. Sockets and switches were positioned as much for discretion as for convenience.

A large fireplace in the sitting room was extant but damp. To salvage it they allowed themselves to break their perfect black box with a new three-tiered ziggurat of reclaimed stone that incorporated the existing hearth and sprouted a black metal flue for a wood-burning stove. The necessary additional lining to the fireplace sat beyond the line of the original exterior. The incongruity is a consequence of the new building having had done to it what had to be done, as it has happened over its lifetime. They added one other element that stepped beyond the rectangle: a small black corrugated metal porch with its own sharply pitched roof. It looks like the kind of porch that such a little building might well have and it fulfils the same function, it keeps out draughts.

The porch's constricted space opens on to the double-height entrance hall. On the right is the stair to the mezzanine landing on which three cupboards contain clothes, a WC and basin, and a shower. A mezzanine 'sleeping area' overlooking the sitting room opens off one side of the landing. On the other is a store that is only accessed by a ladder from the studio. If, as latent 'future-proofing' allows, the building does mutate into a three-bedroom house then this

Croft Lodge Studio, Herefordshire: the new steel stair and structural splints amplify the decay – and the romance – of the surviving timbers.

area will give access to additional rooms above the studio.

The studio and cottage share a dark-grey vinyl sheet floor. Above floor level the studio walls are sharp and clean and the walls in the cottage are gnarled. The extent of dilapidation in the cottage is made clear by the broken ends of old framing timbers and their decay is underlined by the steel nuts and bolts that punctuate their length. One section of timber that was beyond help has been replaced by an undisguised short steel post, which is another incongruity for visitors to ponder. Newness resonates. A new white flush panel door between dining and sitting areas, with a shadow gap between it and the old structure, is blatantly of its own time. How times have changed.

The building, once draughty and chilly, has been blessed with underfloor heating, although the excavation of the existing floor threatened to undermine the existing structure. That source of comfort is, however, for the future, when the building is converted to a full-time dwelling. Connor and Darby presently prefer to rely on two stoves, one in the cottage and one in the studio, which are fed by timber foraged from the woodlands on the Common. Photovoltaic cells on the south-facing roof offset electricity consumption and blend with the black roof.

The project is committed to accepting the consequences of ageing and Connor and Darby both wax poetic about the effect of light on dew-moistened corrugations in the morning and the gentle ageing that is already beginning as plants and algae mellow its edges. In the countryside the fresh and the new look out of place.

Inevitably there had to be new elements within the old. There had to be new upper floor areas and a very simple folded steel stair with a very simple steel balustrade, which turns to protect the edges of the mezzanines. At ground level, a new kitchen with polished steel units is rather high tech, distinctly out of tune with the crumbling plaster and exposed laths of the old walls behind them, as is the white laminate topped table and the moulded plywood chairs.

Other details evolved while work was in progress. There were no satisfactory precedents for how electrical wiring might be fed through the building, or for fixing socket outlets and light switches. Each installation point was considered on its own merits. It helped that the designers/clients lived next door and that problems could be discussed promptly even if decisions did not need to be rushed. Sockets were surface mounted, discreetly located at low level. Light switches are necessarily at eye level or thereabouts and are wittily hidden behind small pieces of hessian fixed on their top edge so that they may be lifted aside when one uses the switch. It is clever but begs a philosophical question: is the introduction of new or the relocation of old

Croft Lodge Studio, Herefordshire: the highly hygienic new kitchen units sit between highly unhygienic existing walls.

rags violating the authenticity of the original fragments? The same principle provides the answer: they are another element that time is, of necessity, adding to the mix.

Like all good country cottages its fireplace is disproportionately large. Connor felt that an existing niche in the chimney breast deserved a bust. This time he did not call on Kapoor but created a ceramic head that looked a little like the faces that appeared in his early drawings and a little like a Giacometti. Its casual execution gives it a semblance of age; it might have been dug up during the excavation of the floor and its tortured expression might lead an archaeologist to presume it to be a juju buried to repel evil. Connor thought enough of it to have a spotlight installed in the niche to illuminate it. He made a few trial pieces and keeps a little collection of them in the recess of the bread oven.

The hybrid of crumbling old and hard-edged new asks a fundamental question about how listed buildings should be treated, and particularly those that are in a state far beyond salvageable. The question is already complicated by increasingly demanding environmental standards that require conversion of a listed building to conform to minimal levels of heat loss and, to achieve that, allow insulation to be attached to its exterior walls. The original continues to exist but cocooned and unseen. Connor and Darby's tin shed provided the protection and left what existed intact, discernable and independent.

Buildings, particularly unimportant little farm buildings, evolve. It is seldom clear what they were in their original state. Connor and Darby recognised the potency of the mix of elements across time when they detailed the necessary new. The steel stair with its flimsiest possible balustrade and handrail is aesthetically as far as one can get, short of resorting to coloured plastics, from the hulking timbers of the old frame. The stainless steel, free-standing kitchen units are the antithesis of the (visually) unhygienic walls that contain them. The rest of the furniture is an appropriately eclectic selection of ageing pieces and a few of Ikea and Muji's better-looking products.

Viewed from the Common the shed becomes a conundrum as the old end wall of the cottage with its posts, beams, laths and crumbling plaster can be seen through the gable window, and that is when the conjunction of shed and ruin comes into its own.

The project's didactic, and aesthetic, worth was immediately recognised. It won the *Architects Journal*'s award for small projects in 2017 and it prompts murmurs of excited incredulity from lecture theatre audiences. Strangely the judges admired it for not 'romanticising the ruin', which is confusing unless they equate romanticising with cosmeticising, which architects might do.[51]

Croft Lodge Studio, Herefordshire: light switches sit discreetly behind found scraps of hessian sacking.

Croft Lodge Studio: the sleeping mezzanine above the sitting room.

Croft Lodge Studio, Herefordshire: twisted, rusted metal window frames suggest that the building was once more than utilitarian.

Croft Lodge Studio, Herefordshire: Connor's howling heads (above and opposite) occupy niches in the old chimney breast.

There are precedents for ruins preserved within new structures but they are cleaned up, made neat; glamorised rather than romanticised. Perhaps the judges were wary of condoning something that might have been seen in the hard-nosed, theorising world of architecture as rather effete. In fact the thought of preserving every found element, however incidental, was as romantic as it was a challenge to the amorphous principles that govern work to old and listed buildings.

It is worth considering the potency of the mix of old and new. Neither cottage nor protecting shed would have won the award on its own and it is wrong to presume, as the judges of an architectural competition would be inclined to do, that credit for their collaborative success lies with the new. If the shed romanticises the ruin, the ruin romanticises the shed. Left to fend for themselves the ruin would be helpless and the shed a minor (because small) architectural triumph. Together they become a great building, after which the urge to tidy up and imply an unknowable history may seem a little irresponsible.

In an interview for the *Architects Journal* after their win was announced, Connor and Darby were asked what set their project apart from the 200 other entries. Darby suggested that while there are many examples of new structures within old buildings, this was a very rare example of old within new. Connor was less rational and talked about the romance of an 'old building hidden inside the new' but qualified that: 'really it is the fact that every detail and surface of the old building has been preserved, which gives a richness and layering to the project'.[52]

The project has been featured widely in magazines and online and caused as much of a stir as Adam Ant's flat did 35 years earlier. It is a found interior that embellishes, and is embellished by, the exterior that contains it. It drips romance without the sentiment that comes with pastiche. The new quasi-agricultural building that protects the broken old shell makes no attempt, other than with the elegance of its detailing, to draw the attention of walkers on the Common who know nothing of the extraordinary idea that brought it into being. It is accepted and it is worth speculating about that acceptance. The pitched roof, the rectangular plan and the vertical window match the diagram of the ideal house that lurks in everyone's imagination but, with great discretion, the studio's ceiling height and the window's height also satisfy the modern taste for light and 'space'.

The collaborative element of the design process is interesting. Connor thought he and Darby had worked together well because they owned and knew they were going to use the building together. She says: 'David pushed for an extreme approach to preservation. I pushed for the quality of the new.'[53] He says: 'I tend to work more intuitively and lack patience. Kate is much more methodical and takes time to work through problems,'[54] which accords with Pierre d'Avoine's conclusion 30-odd years before when he compared his architect's methodology with that of the designers Connor and Powell-Tuck. Their expectations of the award also diverged. Darby, thinking optimistically, hoped that the recognition it brought would bring new clients. Connor said: 'I don't expect anything but it is very nice to have some acknowledgement of your work. It means somebody likes it.'[55]

Croft Lodge Studio, Herefordshire: the conundrum of a decaying ruin within a crisp metal shell is offered to passersby on the common.

paean

A definition of a great designer, or architect, should be that their work is distinguished by its lack of distinguishing features, because every piece should be defined by the specifics of its purpose, its context and its time.

There is a constant in Connor's work but it is that he refuses to, or is incapable of, repeating himself. Where others find a formula and repeat it, he finds something new in every brief and starts afresh.

His work will not slot into the taxonomy of styles. It is not rococo, it is not minimal, nor is it anywhere consistently between. It does not stay still long enough to be pinned down. His projects may be labelled on their particular merits but there is no label that can be attached to the body of work. It could be said to be of the present but it is his present.

The world is full of designers who do exquisite things within a formula they have devised for themselves but they do not cause their peers' jaws to drop. They do not make them think differently. Connor did both those things at the beginning of the 1980s and he is still doing it.

It is easy when one has stylistic consistency to enunciate a 'philosophy'. It is not so easy to be taken seriously when each of one's projects is a law unto itself. And Connor has another problem: his projects have wit and that can make cautious clients, and his duller peers, uneasy.

There is a maxim that says a designer should give a client what they want. Connor does not give them what they want, he gives them what they did not know they wanted – until, that is, he has shown it to them. He needs, and is found by, clients who are a little like him. There may be a force that links iconoclasts, that throws Connor together with McLaren and Westwood and those others who are as inclined as he is to plough their own furrows, who want something extraordinary and know that he can give it to them. One suspects that his threshold for boredom is low and that his favourite projects are those which lead to conclusions that surprise him.

'If all the world were playing holidays, to sport would be as tedious as to work.'[56] But for him work is never tedious if he has a project to get his teeth into. It need not be an outrageous brief because he can find ways to take something as innocent as a small flat and turn it into something that had not crossed anyone else's mind and 40 years later he can rewrite the rules of conservation.

He regrets that he sold so many of his early drawings; they had panache but to make and publish them required bravado. There was nothing like them before but they have had many imitators since. Some of them, the ones he misses most, are of buildings that were never built but which continue to hold their promise and leave room for speculation. The buildings they suggest can be what he wants them to be under violent skies; rooms can be higher and wider and the people who inhabit them disturbingly exotic.

Notes

1. Nick Coombe, interview with the author, 19 September 2019.
2. ibid.
3. David Connor, email to the author, 10 July 2019.
4. ibid.
5. ibid.
6. ibid.
7. ibid.
8. ibid.
9. Anthony Flint, *Modern Man: The Life of Le Corbusier*, New Harvest, 2014.
10. David Connor, email to the author, 10 July 2019.
11. ibid.
12. ibid.
13. George Freeman, interview with the author, London, 3 December 2014.
14. Cited by Sir Hugh Casson, 'Inscape', *Architectural Review*, vol.139, issue 831, 1966, p.334.
15. Ian Latham and Mark Swenarton (eds), 'Jeremy Dixon and Edward Jones: Buildings and Projects 1959–2002', Right Angle Publication Ltd, 2002, p.61.
16. Godfrey Golzen, 'Doing What Architects Used To Do', *RIBA Journal*, vol.92, issue 12, 1985, p.42.
17. Ben Kelly, interview with the author, 10 January 2020.
18. David Connor, conversation with the author, circa 1984.
19. Julian Powell-Tuck, interview with the author, 8 January 2020.
20. Pierre d'Avoinne, interview with the author, 9 July 2015.
21. Nick Coombe, interview with the author, 16 September 2019.
22. Julian Powell-Tuck, interview with the author, 24 June 2015.
23. Godfrey Golzen, 'Doing What Architects Used To Do', *RIBA Journal*, vol.92, issue 12, 1985, p.42.
24. Susana Torre, *Architectural Review*, vol.170, issue 1017, 1981, p.43.
25. Julian Powell-Tuck and David Connor, *Architectural Review*, vol.170, issue 1017, 1981, p.27.
26. Peter York, *Peter York's Eighties*, BBC Books, London, 1995, p.92.
27. *Architectural Review*, vol.170, issue 1017, 1981, p.74.
28. Susana Torre, *Architectural Review*, vol.170, issue 1017, 1981, p.43.
29. Julian Powell-Tuck, interview with the author, 24 June 2015.
30. Julian Powell-Tuck cited by Godfrey Golzen, 'Doing What Architects Used To Do', *RIBA Journal*, vol.92, issue 12, 1985, p.42.
31. ibid.
32. David Connor, interview with the author, 6 September 2019.

NOTES

33 ibid.
34 www.davidconnordesign.co.uk.
35 Nick Coombe, interview with the author, 19 September 2019.
36 BBC News Channel online, 29 April 2010.
37 David Connor, interview with the author, 11 October 2019.
38 ibid.
39 ibid.
40 David Connor, interview with the author, 23 September 2019.
41 ibid.
42 ibid.
43 www.pksarchitects.com.
44 David Connor, interview with the author, 23 September 2019.
45 ibid.
46 Kate Darby, interview with the author, 10 December 2019.
47 Mark Richards, *Hermit Project – Stage 2*, www.markrichards.eu.
48 Adolf Loos, *Architecture*, an essay published in 1910.
49 Kate Darby, interview with the author, 10 December 2019.
50 Peter York, *Authenticity Is a Con*, Biteback Publishing, London, 2014, p.108.
51 *Architects Journal*, 29 March 2017.
52 David Connor, *Architects Journal*, 29 March 2017.
53 Kate Darby, *Architects Journal*, 29 March 2017.
54 David Connor, *Architects Journal*, 29 March 2017.
55 ibid.
56 William Shakespeare, *Henry IV part 1*.

Important teachers

Hugh and Mararget Casson, RCA
Ed Jones, RCA
John Miller, RCA
Fred Scott, RCA
David Wolfe, BSA

Collaborators

Pierre d'Avoine
Ann Bodkin
David Champion
Nick Coombe
Anahi Copponex
Kate Darby
Emily Daye
Mike Delaney
Kate Deneen
Alex Gabrysch
Steve George
Gillian Horn
Karsten Huneck
Anish Kapoor
Ben Kelly
Mark Lintott
Gunner Orefelt
Eva Palme
Julian Powell-Tuck
Mark Richards
Becky Sobell
Sally Stone
Piers Taylor

Image credits

Every effort has been made to identify the authors of the images used in this book. The publisher would be grateful if notified of any amendments or additions needed for future editions. Drawings, unless otherwise indicated, © David Connor, 2020. All rights reserved.

David Connor: 25, 45, 56, 57, 80, 126, 127, 145
Kate Darby: 83, 84, 94, 97, 98, 99, 100
John Linden: 68, 71, 72
Metropolitan Museum of Art: 22 23
James Morris: 129, 130, 135, 137, 139, 140, 141, 142, 143
Stephanie Papalla: 2
Julian Powell-Tuck: 6, 31, 32, 33, 38, 39, 40
Tim Street-Porter: 51, 52, 54, 55
Unknown: 46, 47, 57 (bottom right), 76, 78
Richard Waite: 46 (both), 49, 53

Index

Page numbers in *italics* refer to illustrations

Ant, Adam 30, 36, 38
Architects Journal 138, 143
Architectural Association 30, 41, 86
Architectural Review (*AR*) 34, 35, 36
Bartlett School of Architecture 86, 91
Birmingham Art Gallery 16–17
Birmingham School of Art 17
Bourneville 16, 19, 95
Brown, Capability 50, 117, 121
Casson, Hugh 20
Champion, David 31
Clendinning, Max 19
Connor, David
    family 15–16
    photographs of *2*, *6*
    projects
        Adam Ant's country house *10*, *10*, 36–8
        Adam Ant's flat, London 30–36, *31*, *32*, *33*, 38, 63, 79–80, 96, 114, 144,
        Alice Court, London 65
        Atlantic Bar and Grill, London 75–77, *76*, 81
        Building for a Void, Seville *69*, *71*, *72*, 69–75, 91, 114, 123
        Clarence Hotel, Dublin 77–9
        Connor/Darby flat, London *94*, 95–101, *97*, *98*, *99*, *100*
        Croft Lodge Studio, Herefordshire 124–145, *126*, *127*, *128*, *129*, *130*, *131*, *132*, *135*, *137*, *139*, *140*, *141*, *142*, *143*, *145*
        Descent into Limbo, Kassel 74
        Graphic studio, Los Angeles *56*, *57*, 58
        Hull City of Culture 2017 *13*, *14*
        Hyde Park penthouses, London *61*, *62*, 63
        Kapoor house, Bahamas 101–110, *103*, *104*, *106*, *107*, *109*
        La Ferme Roland, Fréjus, France 88–90, *92–3*
        Le Parc Lord Rendel, Fréjus *89*, 90, 117
        Live! TV, London 81–6, *83*, *84*
        Marco Pirroni's flat *37*, *38*, 38–40, *39*, *40*, 63, 96, 114
        Monsoon 80–81, *80*, 86
        Napa Creek apartments, California *57*
        Primrose Hill flats, London 87–8
        Roppongi nightclub, Tokyo *64*, 65
        Seditionaries, London [World's End] *22*, *23*, 24–8, *25*, *26*, *27*, 79, 110, 113
        Taiwanese projects 63, *66*, 67
        The Floating Hermitage, Croft Castle, Herefordshire 117–124, *118*, *119*, *120*, *122*, *123*, *123*
        Villa Zapu 1984, Napa, California *9*, 41–59, *43*, *44*, *44*, *45*, *46*, *46*, *49*, *51*, *52*, *53*, *54*, *55*, 60, 67, 70, 75, 87, 102, 114, 117
        Vivienne Westwood, Davies Street, London *78*, *78*, *78*, 79–80, 110–113, *111*, *112*
        Will Adams Ecological Centre, Medway Marshes, Kent 114–117, *115*, *116*

Coombe, Nick 12, 30, 42, 70
Copponex, Anahi 124
d'Avoine, Pierre 29–30, 34, 144
Darby, Kate 86, 88–91, 95, 96, 101, 124, 125, 128, 133, 136, 138, 143–4
David Connor Design 67, 81
Golzen, Godfrey 34
Graves, Michael 42–7
Gray, Eileen 19
Grimshaw Architects 69
Hockney, David 20
Hogg, Minn 36
Kapoor, Anish 69–74, 101–110, 138
Kelly, Ben 21–4, 30
Le Corbusier 18, 19, 42
Libera, Adalberto 18–19
Lintott, Mark 63, 67
Loos, Adolf 124, 133
Lundstrom, Thomas 41–2, 102
MacKenzie, Kelvin 82
Malevich 18
McCracken White & Associates 41
McLaren, Malcolm 24–8, 30, 38, 79, 117, 146
Metropolitan Museum of Art, New York 22, 23, 28

Millar, John 20
Orefelt, Gunnar 30, 41, 59, 60–63, 66
P-TCO 30, 58, 59, 60, 63, 65, 67, 69, 75, 88
Palme, Madeleine 38–40
Peyton, Oliver 75–7
Pinhole 63
PKS 86–7
Powell-Tuck, Julian 15, 21, 29–30, 34, 35, 36, 41, 58–9, 60, 63–6, 86, 144
RIBA Journal 21, 34, 59
Richards, Mark 117–121
Royal College of Art (RCA) 12, 19, 20, 29, 31, 34, 41, 50, 66, 70
Royal Institute of British Architects (RIBA) 20, 21, 41, 114
Simon, Peter 80–81
Stefanidis, John 12, 21, 24, 29, 31, 38, 86
Street-Porter, Janet 82, 85
The World of Interiors 36
Torre, Susana 35, 36
Universal Exposition of Seville 69–75
Urmeneta, Juan Bosco Díaz 74–5
van der Rohe, Mies 18
Westwood, Vivienne 24, 28, 38, 79, 110–113, 146